Psychic Palmistry Revealed By Madam Carolyn

Carolyn Ahl

Designed by Roger Ahl and Richard Taecker
Manufactured in the United States of America

ISBN-10: 1-4536-7631-7
EAN-13: 978-1-4536-7631-8
LCCN: 2010911528

With

Love

to

My

Loyal

Clients

CONTENTS

Forward

My name is Carolyn and I am a palm reader. I read palms at Renaissance Festivals around the country as Madam Carolyn. I also read palms via the telephone, the mail and the internet. How do I do this? People send their prints to me by mail, fax or e-mail. I can read palms in person or from prints and either way works.

I have been studying and reading palms since 1969. This is not something that I had planned to do with my life; I was led to it by circumstance. Or, some would say that I was led to a life as a palmist by fate or karma.

I psychically "saw" a burglary for three nights and on the fourth night it occurred. I didn't know what to make of this. I thought that I had made it happen. One of my friends said she thought this might mean that I had had an extra sensory experience, or a psychic vision. This was all new to me, I didn't believe in this stuff. I thought, "What the heck was going on?" I started reading books on intuition and extra sensory perception (ESP), which led me to studying various types of vehicles, such as Astrology, Numerology, Tarot Cards, Runes and then finally, Palmistry.

Learning how to do any type of reading is boring, repetitious and tedious. But when studying palm reading, I was so intrigued with the lines and how they told a story that I couldn't stop. Soon I began reading every hand I could and the rest is history.

My palm reading journey led me to the study of Gypsy folklore as well as the secrets of the Hindu, Oriental and European methods of palmistry. This, and my own keen psychic sense, helped me to develop a style that is all my own.

I have taught palmistry and psychic development for many years. I have written and produced a cassette tape called, *Beginning Palmistry*, which teaches palmistry and includes a booklet of drawings that shows what I am talking about. I have also produced a DVD that teaches Psychic Development. Many of my clients and students have requested that I write a book describing my own methods of psychic palmistry.

This book has information from my *Beginning Palmistry* tape and my DVD, *Psychic Development* in it, but I am adding information on the fingerprints, skin patterns (whorls, arches and circles), the minor lines and how I interpret the many squares, stars, and shapes that appear in the hand. Most of these meanings are my own interpretation and not from any other source.

I would like you to memorize the meanings in this book, and do the exercises I use to both open and close your own intuitive doors. Then take what you learn a step farther and develop your own method of palmistry. It is said that the sign of a good teacher is when their students become better than the teacher. My daughter is a palm reader; she has learned from working with me and through my classes and tapes. She has worked hard, developed her own method of palmistry and is a very fine palmist. Her clients believe that she is better than I am.

This is what I want this book to do for you. I want you to become a dynamite palm reader. I want you to become better than I am.

Even if your ultimate goal is not to become a palm reader; it is interesting and informative to look at your own hands and those of your friends. The psychic exercises that I use and share with you in this book will help you make better decisions and give you a better understanding of yourself.

Introduction to the History of Palm Reading

Palmistry, also called Chiromancy (meaning hand divination), dates back thousands of years. It is an art to some, a science to some and it is reviled as a fake by others. Popular theory has palmistry originating in India and coming to Europe with the nomadic tribes of Gypsies as they traveled throughout Europe and Asia. However, in prehistoric caves in Spain and France there are hands painted on the walls of the caves with the major lines drawn in great detail. Archaeological finds have uncovered hands of ivory, stone and wood made by ancient civilizations. Ancient writings about the practices and principles of reading hands have been found in India and Asia.

I met a Korean man who said he studied palmistry texts in a monastery in Korea that were written on animal skin with what he assumed was blood. He said the skins were so ancient he was afraid of ripping them as he turned the pages. Remarkably, his knowledge of the lines of the palm is very similar to mine.

I believe all cultures have had some type of palm reading and that palmistry doesn't come from one era or part of the world.

In ancient times Buddhist Priests read the hands and feet of children when they were born. There are prints of the baby Buddha's foot patterns that were taken when he was born and from these the priests prophesized that he would become a great leader.

One of the most celebrated palmists in the 19th century was the French woman Marie-Anne le Normand. She was a palmist and Tarot reader and one of her clients was Josephine de Beautharnais, who later married Napoleon Bonaparte. She prophesied a glittering military career for him during a reading for Josephine. She said that he would become the most famous man in France. Obviously her predictions came true. Later she was imprisoned by Napoleon for predicting that he would divorce Josephine. He apparently let her out after the divorce was final.

Count Louis Hamon, was a palm reader in the early 20th century. He used the name, Cheiro, (from the Greek word for 'hand') when he read palms and he was famous in his day. He wrote, *The Language of the Hand*, which is still in print today. He was also psychic as he foretold the future with remarkable accuracy during his palm readings. According to one biographer, Prince Edward, Joseph Chamberlain, General Kichener, Sarah Bernhardt, Mark Twain, Oscar Wilde and other famous people were Cheiro's clients. He is still one of the best known palmists today.

Palmistry really became popular in the 19th century when more books on Palmistry were published and more people had access to them. Palmistry continues to be fascinating to this day.

CHAPTER 1

MY BEGINNING

When I began doing readings I used the dominant hand, the one you write with, as the hand that shows what you are currently doing with your life and the non-dominant hand as your possibilities, or what you were born with.

There are some readers who read this way. Other palmists use the non-dominant hand exclusively, or the dominant hand exclusively. They see whatever they need for a reading in one palm.

I read every book I could get my hands on, memorized the meanings of the lines and the shapes of the hand. I met an American Indian woman who taught me what her grandmother had taught her. I also had my hand read by other palmists to see how they did their readings.

As I became more comfortable with my knowledge of the lines, I talked everyone I knew into letting me read their hands. I got excited about my growing skills and got excellent feedback from my readings. Then a friend of mine talked me into reading palms at a fair where I would need to charge a fee and since it was her booth, she took half. I felt it was too early for me to read for people other than my friends and I wasn't comfortable charging money for readings. She talked me into it and since I felt that I wasn't giving my clients enough information; at the end of each reading I would clasp my client's hand, connecting the web of skin between my thumb and first finger with the web of skin between their thumb and first finger. I would close my eyes and take a deep breath. Surprisingly, I started seeing visions that were very specific. I told one lady that I saw her standing with her hands on her hips and glowering at a wringer washing machine that was broken. She told me that is why she came to the fair; she couldn't do her laundry. You can tell how long ago this was as wringer washing machines are almost antiques today.

I quit doing this after one fair because, after a few days of doing readings I started to hear a high frequency buzzing up near the ceiling. This was a fourteen day show and I was reading for several hours each day. The buzzing started on the 5th day and at first it sounded like a mosquito. A day or so later it sounded like a wasp. The following day it sounded like a phonograph record at high speed and the next day it became a record at slow speed. Fortunately the show ended, and I did not read for the public again until I knew what this was and how to turn it off. I learned that this is a discarnate (meaning having no body, form or substance) voice that was beginning to speak to me. In the psychic world it is called Clairaudience and is considered a form of channeling.

I will show you the exercises and visualizations that I use to control this type of psychic phenomena in Chapter 18.

Once I had read for a person I never wanted to read them again. I believed I had told them all I could about their hands. But people wanted to come back to me and when I read them again, I saw that some of their lines had changed.

I didn't think the major lines could ever change, but over the forty years I have been a palmist I have discovered that they do. They change over years. I even argued this point with a policeman who was a fingerprint specialist. He said none of the lines ever change just like fingerprints never change. I showed him minor lines that were appearing while I was reading him.

I discovered that the minor lines change quickly, and I noticed that when I was looking at them, some lines got darker or would turn red and sometimes new lines would appear. I also noticed that parts of the palm would become warmer and lines popped out at me when I touched them. I began to read those areas, and my clients would acknowledge that what I was seeing was correct. I was seeing real, current events in their lives. This was exciting.

This information turned out to be accurate. As time passed, I found what I was seeing was accurate for predicting the future. I want to add here that no person, or psychic, can be 100% accurate. My accuracy is high, but it can't be 100%. If I were able to see the future that accurately it wouldn't be good for me or my client. What would be the point of living if you knew everything that would occur in your life? It would be like reading a book that you've read before. When I read for you I can give you a peek into your probable future. I can tell you what is most likely to happen if you continue in the direction you are going. I can also tell you that this is changeable, that you can change your future.

As I continued reading for people I began hearing an inner voice telling me what to say to some of my clients. I remember the first time this happened. I was telling a lady that I saw her dating someone she was beginning to fall in love with and I heard an inner voice saying, "Tell her he is married." I did and she was shocked and so was I. It turned out he was married and she was able to save herself some heartbreak by breaking up with him right away. Pictures began to form in some peoples hands when I was reading them and when I would tell them what I saw, the pictures would disappear.

I read the entire hand, both hands and then I let my client ask questions. I rarely ask questions; if I do it is to clarify something I see. When I am done with the reading, it is like a light goes off.

I believe we all have a shield or psychic barrier around us. I have one and you have one. I read up to the shield and not farther. When I read for someone we form a bond of trust, our shields become thin and we develop a connection that allows me to see things quicker and with more clarity.

Before we begin to look at a person's hand it is important to review what I call the

Rules of Palmistry

To be a good palmist you must genuinely like people. It is the most intimate form of reading as there is physical contact between you and your client. They are inviting you to look into their hands and thus, their lives. This lays bare their hopes and dreams, as well as their fears and failures. It is important that you are ethical, loving and kind.

I interpret the lines in the most positive way possible. If there are negative lines or events that I see, I show my clients how to overcome them. Your responsibility as a palm reader is huge. People remember what you say. I remember a lady that I read for saying, "When I was fifteen a palm reader told me I would be married five times. I've been married four times and I'm waiting for my fifth." Now there was nothing on her hand that indicated she'd be married five times. Her hands showed a strong need to please others and this can mean multiple marriages, because she could see other people's needs and desires stronger than she could see her own. This type of person is easily influenced by other people's desires and needs. This became a self-fulfilling prophecy. She heard it and she made it happen. If someone uses my reading for a self-fulfilling prophecy, I want it to be a positive prophecy leading to a positive future.

You are entering a field where your words carry weight and I can't impress upon you enough that you need to be very careful how you phrase your words. Be positive. Use positive phrases. Words can mean the difference between hope and despair.

I often trade readings. One time I had two astrologers who owed me readings so I decided to go to them both on the same day. Astrology shouldn't leave too much open to interpretation as the planets would all be in the same place on that day.

One astrologer phrased things in a way that left me feeling like crawling out of her office and the other phrased things in a way that made me feel hopeful for the future.

That day the planets were aligned in such a way that one reader said I may have to institutionalize a family member and the other interpreted it to mean I would change one of my kid's schools. Both were reading the institution aspect correctly, but the change of schools was actually accurate and much more positive. So, while you are learning the meanings of palm reading, bone up on your vocabulary as well, and remember that your words are important. They carry weight. I know I've said this twice, but it is important.

Try to moderate your voice so it is upbeat and positive. Talk in a soft voice.

14

CHAPTER 2

BEGINNING
THE VOYAGE

Some readers make prints of the palms and read these prints. It is true that much detail comes out with a print and you can record changes in the hand by taking prints from year to year. I prefer to have the person in front of me, but I also read with prints and photos that are faxed, mailed or e-mailed and I get psychic impressions from them as well.

I read both hands during my readings. I read the present from their lines and then go to future possibilities, psychically. I stay within a one or two year period of time for my predictions. People want to know what is happening to them now, not ten years ago or ten years from now. There are areas in the hands that show deep seated memories. The memory can be deep grief as from the loss of a loved one, or it can be a lighter grief, such as disappointment by parents, friends or job. Stored emotions will show in the palms, and if the past is bothering my client, it will stand out. I will talk about how to let these old emotions go.

I start my readings by holding both of my client's hands with one hand and using the fingers of my other hand to feel the texture of their hands and to press on the lines. This will make some lines pop out or change color. Pay attention to the lines that pop out as they are the current events.

I mentioned before that I read both hands. I do this because I have found that each hand is an important element in seeing where you are and where you are going with your life.

Remember, even though I am separating the hand into individual parts to teach you how to interpret the hands, I read the entire palm, going over the shape and texture of the palms as well as the lines and mounts.

When you are looking at palms, go slowly and carefully examine their lines. Take the time to touch their hands. Think of reading hands as an investigation into the person you are reading. You are reading the book of their life. You will be examining the shape of the palms, the fingers and their shape, the lines, the mounts and the feel of the person you are reading. There is a wealth of detail in each person's palms; you are looking for what makes them unique.

No two hands are the same, even when on first glance they may seem the same.

In palmistry you look for lines that stand out and are different. You don't ignore lines and markings that are average. You do read them, but you are looking for lines and markings that are unique to the person you are reading. You are looking for the unusual in the hand. This is especially true when examining the size and shapes of the fingers.

Never feel that you or your clients are doomed because of a weak hand or a weak line. There will often be strengths in other lines in the hand or in the fingers that compensate for this. Aristotle was said to have had his hand read by a student who pointed out that he had many lines showing weaknesses. He said, "Yes, but look at what I have overcome." A good palmist will point out the way to compensate for any lines or shapes that show weakness in their client's hands.

Shape and Texture

Imagine you are sitting across from me. I take a deep breath to center myself and then I begin by holding your hands. I run my thumb across the palm of first one of your palms and then the other. My fingers are on the backs of your hands and I am feeling the texture. I ask myself questions. Is the palm springy or is it slightly soft? Is it so soft that it feels as if there are no bones in the palm? Do the palms feel hard, supple, soft, springy or coarse? Is the hand large or is it small? How does the hand length compare to the size of the face? What shape is the palm and how does its length compare to the length of the fingers? These are the first things to look at when you are reading a palm and the answer to each question is important in your reading of the hand.

A springy, supple hand means high energy; this is someone who embraces life, enjoys physical activity, but doesn't crave it. This is someone who is influenced to a degree by their surroundings. The springier hand is a person who is a thinker and also a doer.

A soft hand is a creative person who doesn't have as much vitality or energy. They are affected by the atmosphere and temperature and almost anything else around them. They are thinkers, but they do not turn their thoughts into action as easily as the springy hand.

A hand that feels spongy, as if there are no bones in it, is an indolent hand. This is often a brilliant hand. The person who owns this hand can be physically lazy but mentally very active. These people are easily influenced by the barometer and are sensitive to changing temperatures.

A firm hand is someone who is lusty and has a surging energy that continues on and on, regardless of temperature, emotions or outside influence. This person is athletic and has tremendous stamina. This is also someone who can be inflexible.

A hand that has a hollow center is a peace loving person. This is someone who may go to great lengths to keep the peace. It is also someone who doesn't show or express feelings well. But, as a peacemaker, they can hold the world in the palm of their hand. This person can be very influential.

If the hand is moderately springy, yet somewhat firm, just file this in the back of your mind and keep examining the hand. This is a person who has moderate energy and a good balance in their life. They color within the lines in the coloring book of their life, most of the time. We are looking for abnormalities in the hands. Those are the parts of the hand we will read.

A person who has a narrow palm sees their own point of view before others. It is someone who does not always have sympathy for others.

A wide palm is someone who likes to be out in the open air. It is someone who is tolerant of others and has a lot of patience.

A flat palm is combative and stands up for themselves and others.

But, remember, we are reading the entire hand. Intelligence is found in all parts of the hand. The spongy hand is not the only place to find brilliance, nor is the spongy hand always lazy.

Now turn the palms over. Look at the pores of the skin. Large pores belong to someone who has natural stamina. They can push their physical bodies with little or no side effects. A person with fine textured skin that looks like porcelain is someone who needs to pay attention to their body. These people need to get adequate sleep. They must pay attention to what foods they are eating. Their internal systems are delicately balanced and if they overuse their body they will become ill. This doesn't mean that they are prone to illness; they just need to take better care of themselves than someone with coarser pores.

If we have a person who has a firm, springy palm with fine textured skin, then I don't read either, as these characteristics will cancel each other out. This is someone who has more energy and is not so delicately balanced.

If we have a person with fine textured skin and a long narrow palm that is soft and spongy, I would tell them that they do need to take better care of themselves and get more exercise to get the best use of their body. I also tell them to make lists to help them take their ideas from thought to action.

A medium textured hand is someone who is balanced. They can go without tiring longer and need less sleep. They can push their limits with only moderate side effects. They are basically well balanced people.

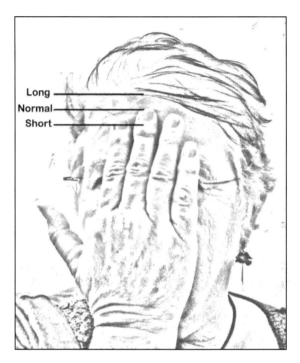

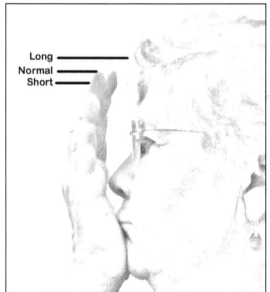

Size Does Matter

The distance from the wrist of the hand to the tip of the middle finger should be about the same length as the face. To measure this, put your wrist to your chin. Your middle finger should be about a quarter of an inch below your hair line. If it is longer or shorter than this, the person owning this hand has some special characteristics.

The Length of the Hand.

A small hand is someone who likes large projects, someone who is a quick thinker and likes to have many projects going at the same time. This is someone who would do well to have another person organize things, or clean up after them, as they get impatient and irritated with details. They often act on impulse. But they are dreamers who can make their dreams come true.

A large hand is a person who pays meticulous attention to details, but they don't get so caught up in small details that they can't see the larger picture. They often like to work with small objects. A large hand is someone who is organized and thinks things through before acting. They take charge and are often executives.

A hand that is the normal length has a balance between thought, and action and their energy flows evenly. They have characteristics of both the small hand and the large hand.

Hand Shapes

The hand is generally divided into five shapes.

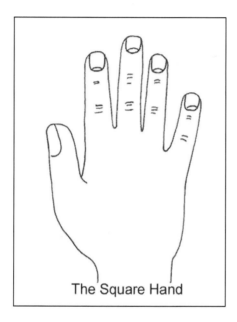

The Square Hand

The square hand is an orderly person who rarely acts on impulse. They are methodical and are the salt of the earth. They are dependable and cope well under pressure. They think things through and may seem slow; but they are not. Once their mind is made up it is difficult to change it. This person has the ability to cope with life's challenges.

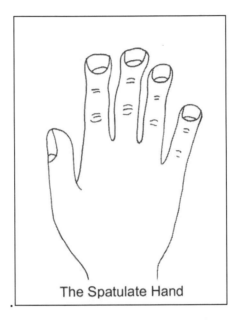

The Spatulate Hand

The spatulate hand is broad and strong. They are realists. The visual quality is a splaying out of the hand from the base and the tips of the fingers splay out as well. These people are action oriented. They are creative and impulsive. They are often extroverted and they can grasp situations and solutions simultaneously.

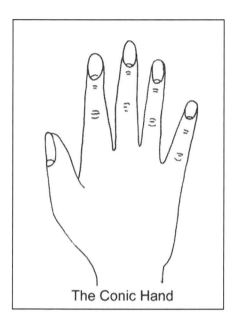

The Conic Hand

The conic hand is a person who is receptive to feelings and ideas. The hands are tapered at the fingers and at the base. They are artistic and can be impulsive. They begin projects and don't always complete them. They are often dreamers and don't follow through.

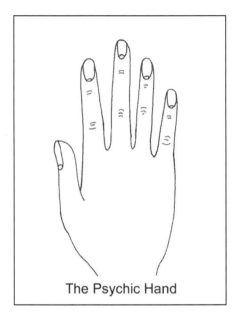

The Psychic Hand

The psychic hand is a rare hand. It is most often seen in women and the hand is beautifully formed with long graceful fingers with pointed tips. These people are motivated by feelings and intuition. They have vivid imaginations and are usually creative. They are high strung and easily influenced or manipulated by others. They have wonderful creative ideas but often lack the ability to initiate action.

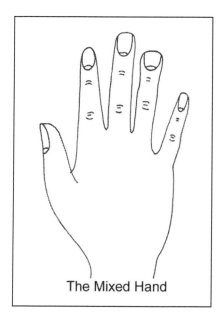

The Mixed Hand

The mixed hand is the most common type of hand that you will see. This hand combines the aspects of all the other hands. The palms are often more rounded and the fingertips are mixed. For instance, you may see two fingertips conic and the other two square.

The mixed hand has stability. They have a nice blend of thought and action. There is creativity, and intuition with stability. This is someone who will get the job done.

CHAPTER 3

LET YOUR FINGERS DO THE TALKING

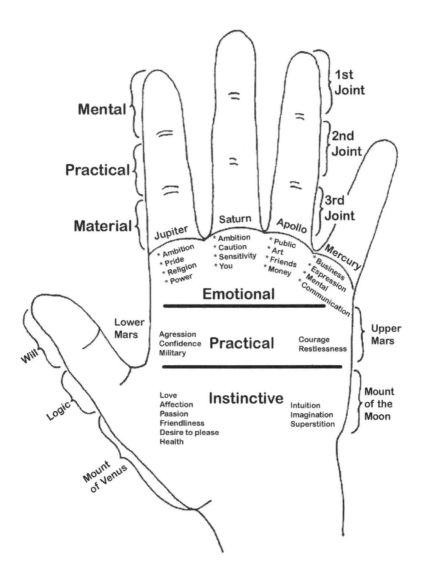

Fingers Have Names

The fingers are named Jupiter, Saturn, Apollo and Mercury. These names come from the Greek tradition of palmistry which named the fingers after their Gods. A way to remember this is JSAM or jzam.

The thumb is always called the thumb.

Each segment of the finger is called a phalange.

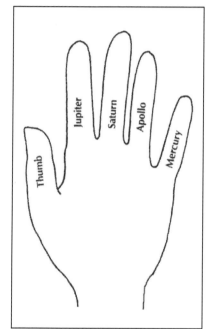

Ask the client to hold their hands up, palms towards you. If the fingers seem all bunched together, and the thumb is tucked in towards the palm, this is someone who holds things close to their chest. They have a harder time opening up and sharing themselves. It shows a shy nature. Even if the entire hand is outgoing and boisterous, their inner nature guards their emotions.

If the forefinger, the Jupiter finger, slants towards the middle finger, or Saturn, this is someone who likes to acquire or collect things. If the Saturn finger slants towards Jupiter, this is someone who throws things out when they don't need them anymore.

If all the fingers slant towards Saturn, this is someone with a thoughtful nature. They think things through before they act.

If all of the fingers slope towards Mercury, the little finger, this is someone who speaks before they think. If the fingers all slope towards the Jupiter finger, it is someone who needs to curb their ego. I would say to this person: "you will attain influence over other people. This can be influence over people through your career, or influence over your family, but it is important for you to be kind and caring when you make decisions."

I would not usually say, "Be careful that your ego doesn't destroy you," as the person's ego may be tempered by all the other lines in the hand. But ego can destroy if it is unchecked.

When the hand is held up and all the fingers splay outward or are widely separated, this is a person who is outgoing and generous.

If the Jupiter and Mercury finger seem to fall away from the Saturn and Apollo fingers which then stay close together, this is someone who is good at speaking their mind. They think fast and have excellent command of language. This person would not think, "Oh, I should have said this," after an argument. They would have their words ready to argue their point. They also have the ability to lead others.

When reading palms we look for fingers that are not the normal length and width for the hand.

Always keep in mind; we are looking for the parts of the client's hand that make them different from everyone else. Interpreting these make the reading tailored for the individual.

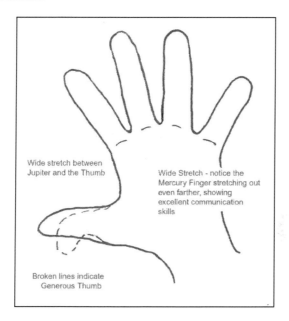

Wide stretch between Jupiter and the Thumb

Wide Stretch - notice the Mercury Finger stretching out even farther, showing excellent communication skills

Broken lines indicate Generous Thumb

A wide stretch between the Jupiter finger and the thumb indicates generosity. If the tip easily bends back they are mentally flexible, but tend to be overly generous. They may have problems holding on to their money. This can also indicate dramatic talent.

If they hold their thumb close to their palm, they are less able to be flexible. They are careful with money. This is a more formal person. It can take time to get close to them.

A narrow stretch is someone who doesn't take risks, and can be somewhat miserly with their money and their emotions.

The Thumb Rules

The thumb is the most important of all the fingers as it reflects willpower.

Hold the thumb and the first finger, or Jupiter, together. Imagine a line dividing the first segment or phalange of the Jupiter finger in half. Determine where the tip of the thumb falls in relation to this line.

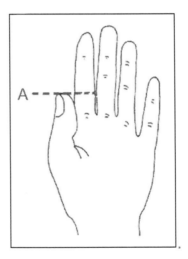

Here the thumb terminates at A. This is the most common length. You understand where you fit in the world. You have good energy, good judgment, and are an active person. You are a thinker and a doer.

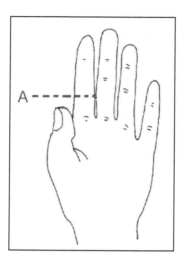

Here the thumb terminates below A. When you have a shorter thumb you have a lack of ambition. You are intelligent, and love to do projects because you are interested in them, and not because they are the latest fad. You do things for the love of doing, and not always for material gain. You may make money with your ideas, and projects, but that isn't your main objective. You are intuitive. There are times when you don't finish what you start.

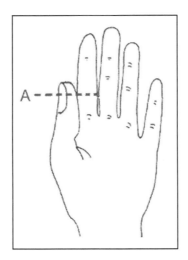

Here the thumb terminates above A. When you have a long thumb you have tremendous will and sense of consequence. You reach high peaks in life. You have a definite drive to succeed. You have the ability to get your ideas across, whether by writing or speaking. The long thumb is an intelligent thumb.

It was said you could recognize Cervantes, who wrote *Don Quixote*, from across the street by the length of his thumb. He is remembered as a very intelligent man and he was larger than life.

Hold the thumb and the little finger, Mercury, together. They are usually the same length, even when they are considered long or short when measured to the Jupiter finger.

Jupiter

The Jupiter finger is an important part of a palm reading. It shows self-respect, power, desire for glory and recognition. It shows money and selfishness. It is about you, your self-worth, and how you portray yourself to others.

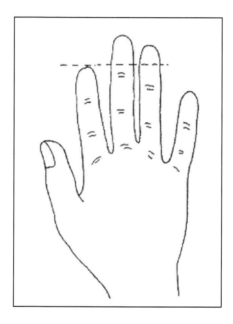

Compare the length of the Jupiter finger to the Apollo finger. Above, the Jupiter finger is slightly shorter than the Apollo finger. This shows a lack of ego, or sense of self.

People with this formation will start confidently, but lose steam quickly, as their self-esteem falters. They struggle to keep learning, and they are hard workers, yet they do not rest on their accomplishments. They continually strive to do better and they work harder than other people, as they never believe they are good enough.

Therefore, these are often the very people who succeed and do great things. If your Jupiter finger is shorter than the Apollo finger you won't go on an ego trip, or become so sure of yourself that you can't look at your mistakes and learn from them. This lack of ego can be good for people in positions of power, as this means they won't become a tyrant.

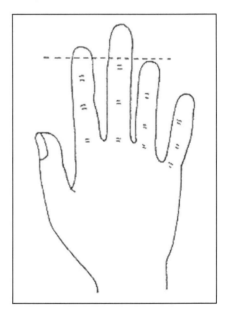

Here the Jupiter finger is longer than the Apollo finger. When this finger is only slightly longer it shows a healthy ego. These people rarely lose confidence in themselves or their ideas. These are people who love to be in control, and will often gravitate to a leadership position. They don't like to lose. They often go into politics. Long Jupiter fingered people are responsible individuals.

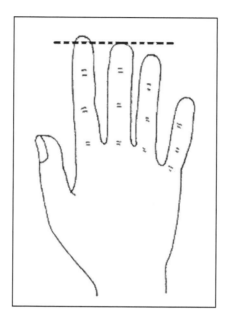

When the Jupiter finger is considerably longer than the Apollo finger, it is called the Napoleonic finger. The danger of becoming a tyrant is present and a person with this finger will need to watch for that tendency. This is a rare formation. Napoleon was said to have had an extremely long Jupiter finger.

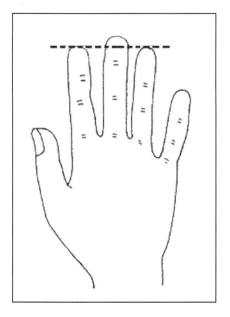

If the Jupiter finger and the Apollo finger are the same length, this is someone who has a rare vision of life. They are likely to be fussy in their likes and dislikes. These people feel physical discomfort easily, and they are vulnerable to heat and cold. They can be jealous, and do not share themselves easily.

Saturn

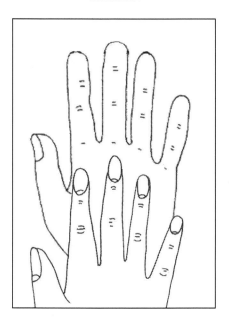

The length of your middle finger, or the Saturn finger, should be 7/8th of your palm. The Saturn finger is the finger of spirituality; it is how you view your inner self. It is the subconscious and it is how you see yourself. The Saturn finger shows your mental boundaries and the qualities that make up your values. It is what keeps you on the path of following the laws of society. This finger is about your soul and your spiritual beliefs. This is not what religion you follow, rather how you follow the religion you embrace. If the Saturn finger is particularly long, you take life seriously. You are rigid in following rules and care a great deal about doing what you consider the 'right' thing. If it is extremely long, raising a digit above the Jupiter and Apollo finger, there is a tendency to be morbid and to look at the negative side of

life. Depending on other things in the hand, this can indicate depression.

If the Saturn finger is short it can indicate a tendency to
be disorganized and this person is easily affected by
stress.

Apollo

The Apollo finger is the ring finger. It shows love of
beauty and artistic sensitivities. It shows the possible
artistic abilities that you can develop. It shows how you
interact with others. The Apollo finger shows how we
create a home for ourselves.

A long Apollo finger can be a critical person. This is
someone who has an extraordinary desire for glory,
fame and fortune. This can be an excellent quality, but it
may be someone who will do anything for fame or
wealth, and not care what type of body count they leave
in their wake. I look for indications of good character in
other parts of the palm when I see this. I point out to my
client that everything has a price or reckoning, and that
it is important to be honorable in dealing with others.
This can also indicate a love of gambling and risk taking.
This is a sporting person, and they enjoy flirting. They
like to bask in attention.

A short Apollo finger is rare. It leaves a person with a
very limited ability to enjoy the beautiful things in life.

Mercury

The Mercury finger is the little finger and it rules communication. Communication works both ways; it shows
how you reach others with your spoken, or written skills,

and how you understand others when they communicate with you.

Usually Mercury fingers come to the second digit on the Apollo finger. However, sometimes the Mercury finger sits very low on the hand and it just looks shorter than normal.

Long Mercury fingers indicate a gift for oration. Such people have a gift of speech, they are good with language, and that includes the written language, as well as the spoken language. They can twist their listeners around their fingers. They are clever. They are often good with money. The long Mercury finger indicates a quick wit and a charming personality.

A short Mercury finger indicates a person who doesn't always understand what someone is saying to them. They may be very literal and don't read between the lines when someone is talking to them. They are usually very smart and do well with the written language. They have difficulty finding the correct words to express themselves when speaking.

I don't read the crooked Mercury finger as negative as so often this is genetic. A crooked Mercury finger is supposed to be someone who bends the truth, but I haven't found this to be accurate.

How Fingers Fit in the Scheme of Things

Have your client hold their palms up in front of you. When all the fingers lean towards the middle of the hand, this is a person with a serious nature. This person is receptive to others and they are idealistic.

If all the fingers slope towards the thumb, this is a person with a materialistic nature. If all the fingers slope towards Mercury, this is a person who has a great need for freedom in their life.

If the fingers slope forward, the person is insecure.

If the fingers are straight, this is someone who has a harmonious nature and a balanced state of mind.

When the fingers of the hand are supple and turn backwards easily the client is mentally flexible and has a quick wit. Likewise, stiff fingers belong to someone who has trouble changing their minds.

Short fingers belong to people who think quickly and who jump to conclusions. This isn't always bad as their quick mind assimilates information fast and their conclusions are often very accurate.

Long fingers belong to people who think in the abstract, they are analytical and detail orientated. If a person has a large hand and short fingers, they have some characteristics of each type and the negative is usually cancelled out.

Digits and Bulges

Bulges on the finger joints are called knots. These knots show the time between thought and action, providing they are not from injury or arthritis. A short fingered person with knots on their finger joints would be less likely to act on impulse. Smooth fingers do not impede thought.

In the lore of palm reading, knots slow thought down. People with knots think things through and look at things from every angle before they act.

Likewise, smooth finger joints would belong to someone who acts more intuitively and doesn't think things through.

The above statement may apply to some extent. But age and injuries change the finger joints, and some people who are very impulsive have thick finger joints and vice versa. Take some time to explore this for yourself. When you are examining the hands of your friends or your clients, feel the knots. Ask them questions about how they perceive their thought process. This is how you will learn the art of palm reading. Studying, and asking questions. You will keep the information that works for you and discard what doesn't.

I do feel the knots when I read palms, especially the Jupiter finger's first knot. If this is more developed than the rest of the knots, it is someone who is good with money. They usually earn a lot of money or will earn a lot of money.

You can only read the finger joints at the first and second phalange. The first finger joint is read as part of the first phalange and the second finger joint as part of the second phalange.

Each finger normally has three sections. These are called phalanges. A fourth phalange is rare but does occur. This is most common on the Mercury finger.

The first phalange is the nail phalange. It denotes the mental attributes of that finger. This shows how you identify with your religion, your spirituality and yourself.

The second phalange is the practical, or intellectual. This indicates determination and strength of character.

The third is the physical or the material. This indicates sensuality and passion for food, sport, sex and home.

The three phalanges should be equal in length and thickness.

Fingers where all the phalanges are roughly equal are balanced phalanges. They show harmony of spirit and action.

If you see a phalange that is markedly different from its mates, this is the phalange you would read.

It is rare to see a fourth phalange but when you do it is usually found on the Mercury finger. It is supposed to mean a rare ability to communicate with others, but I don't find this true. I find that this is someone who becomes a good communicator as they get older. When the person is young they are often shy when expressing their opinions or they stumble for words, especially when stressed. I have never seen a line that denotes stuttering, so this doesn't mean that the person will stutter.

Under each third phalange is a chained line that separates the fingers from the palms. Usually there is one line on Jupiter and Saturn and two lines on Apollo and Mercury. If you have a double chained line under Jupiter this is read as management ability or a drive to own a business. The double chained line on Saturn is a tendency towards melancholy and today that is called depression. Single lines on Apollo and Mercury are not read.

The double lines on Apollo show a creative person who usually has several artistic talents. The double lines on Mercury mean someone who thinks fast and speaks fast.

Jupiter Finger Phalanges

A long first phalange on the Jupiter finger indicates religious feelings, or more broadly speaking, psychological tendencies; for the word religion embraces much more than the church. For instance, a long first segment, or phalange, on the Jupiter finger would belong to someone who is likely to go into a religious order. They would do this, not for the glory of God, but to feel superior to others. Perhaps the same man doesn't go into a religious order; perhaps he becomes a scientist or a baker. Again, that need to let work become a religion would come to the surface. As a scientist he may discover something useful to mankind but sell it to a company who would not use it. A baker might skimp on sanitary requirements to increase profits. These people don't really care about others, they have large egos. But remember, the lines on the palms can moderate this.

The second phalange is that of ambition and self-advancement. A long second phalange is a person who could become a one faceted person.

A long third phalange on the Jupiter finger indicates the love of power. If this phalange is ultra-thick it can lead to over indulgence in things of the flesh. That means food, sex, drink, drugs. In this case, you would like to see some really strong lines in this person's hand and a really strong thumb.

Short phalanges indicate a lack of the above characteristics. This isn't a bad thing, as a short phalange tempers negative characteristics.

Saturn Finger Phalanges

A long first phalange denotes a leaning towards melancholy. It indicates sadness in the temperament. A short phalange indicates less of a leaning towards melancholy.

A long second phalange shows a love of plants, gardening, and agriculture. This can mean care in the growing of relationships with people, animals or plants. A short phalange is someone who wouldn't want to be bothered with planting seeds but would buy the plant. However, they may toss it out if it droops.

A long third phalange indicates economy; if it is quite long it is someone who doesn't part with his money. We all know people who always let you pick up the check. Well, take a look at their third phalange.

A short third phalange is someone who spends money, not always on others, but on themselves.

Apollo Finger Phalanges

A long first phalange indicates a love of art and of beauty. This is a person who collects art and loves being surrounded with beautiful things.

A long second phalange means an intellectual appreciation of art. Artists with this characteristic will not only paint or sculpt, but they will study art history and the lives of the great masters to learn how they developed their art.

A short second phalange is someone who tends to be insecure and often over compensates. They exaggerate their own self-worth, bragging to make up for low self-esteem.

A long third phalange shows a love of riches, a fondness for displays of wealth and much personal vanity. If the phalange is also thick, it means that possessions would become an overriding passion and could be negative as this could be a thief or someone who hoards.

A medium third phalange with a long second phalange on the Apollo finger would mean that this person would buy what they could afford, and think nothing of sharing what they have with friends.

Mercury Finger Phalanges

A long first phalange is someone who is eloquent when speaking. They have a pleasing voice and are often in the public eye as teachers, politicians or orators. If extremely long, it is someone who stretches the truth or exaggerates.

A long second phalange indicates a scientific mind and this person loves to share their discoveries. They often write and teach.

A long third phalange belongs to the diplomat. This is someone who doesn't need to search for the right word in an argument. If this phalange is really long, this person can be a schemer.

Short phalanges would negate these tendencies. Impatience comes into play with the short phalanges. For instance, a short third phalange person wouldn't be a good schemer as they lack the patience to pull off a scheme. They are often not diplomatic because they can't be bothered.

Thumb Phalanges

The first phalange, the nail phalange, shows strength of will, dependability and firmness of character. If it is too long it is someone who has a tendency to be despotic. If short, it leads to indecision, yet they can be obstinate. If it is short and has a thick ball on the pad you will have a hard time convincing this person, as they are often very stubborn. Being obstinate and stubborn isn't necessarily a bad quality. It gives the person staying power. That can indicate success, as these people never give up. If they have the type of hand that allows them to think things through or they make intuitive decisions, this works for them. But, if they are the type of person who doesn't think things through, and their intuition isn't as good; I advise these people to check out all their options before they hunker down and get obstinate. Sometimes flexibility is the way to go before the decision is made, and then being stubborn afterwards is good.

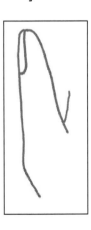

If the first phalange is broad and the thumb pad is flat to an unusual degree, you have someone who holds onto anger and stuffs their emotions. They will stuff emotions for a long time and then blow up about something that has nothing to do with what is going on. During a reading I tell these people that this is a waste of energy. They need to learn to know how they feel at the moment. I also tell these people that they need to learn to talk about how they feel, using, "I," words. Usually they will get mad and say, "You did that," to their friends, spouse, or children. They tend to blame others for their feelings. Learning to speak in, "I feel," or, "I don't like this," or "that makes me angry," helps them own their anger, which makes their lives and the lives of those they love, easier. If the majority of the lines are red and angry looking, I emphasize that being angry is OK; but it is their anger and they need to deal with it.

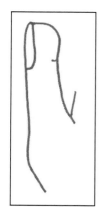 If the pad on the first phalange is puffy and bulbous, it is called the murderer's thumb, or the club thumb. This is not someone who is a murderer. I find this thumb is a genetic trait. Usually this is a person who is intuitive but can act on impulse. This type of intuition is usually felt in the body, as in a tingling on the arms, or a feeling of their hair standing on end. You may have heard the saying, "By the pricking of my thumbs." People with this thumb often feel their intuition this way. I haven't found people with this thumb prone to violence. I have found this type of thumb on men and women of all races. Most people with this thumb recall a family member who also has this thumb, so I believe it is a genetic type of intuition.

The second phalange is the phalange of logic and reasoning. A long second phalange is someone who thinks things through. If it is short they are more likely to act first and think later. When it is thick there is a tendency to be outspoken.

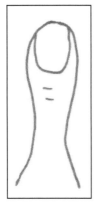

If the second phalange of the thumb is wasp-waisted, or looks like it is caving in at the sides, this is someone who is naturally very tactful. They are able to finesse people and are good in settling complaints.

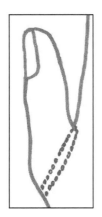

Some palmists consider the small chained area below the second phalange, the third phalange. Others consider the Mount of Venus the third phalange. I use the small chained area, shown in the picture, as the third phalange. Most people have some type of formation under the second phalange. This is the joint of the thumb and this area tells about education. When I read this part of the hand, I use my fingers to feel the elasticity, or fullness of the joint. If it has a nice solid feeling and it has a double chain formation, this is a person who loves to learn and is always in some type of class. If there is only one chain on the joint, it isn't someone who doesn't like to learn, but they prefer to learn on their own. If it is a large area, and has heavy chaining, it is someone who loves to argue and will argue just for the fun of it. Or, as my father said to me, "You would argue with a fence post."

There are some readers who use the fleshy mount under the thumb as the third phalange, but I don't. This is the Mount of Venus, and I read this later in the palm reading.

Finger Tips

Fingertips have their own story and they are important to the reading.

Pointed tips are rare. When you do see them, it is someone who is easily excited; they have a lot of nervous energy and they are extremely intuitive. They are people who are affected by other people's energy and they are also affected by weather pressures. Barometer changes can make them feel as if something awful is going to happen.

People with rounded fingertips are people with a sensible approach to life, are moderately sensitive to the atmosphere and other people's energy.

Square tips are people who are practical. Flared tips or spatulate tips belong to a person who is skilled with their hands. They are very precise when they work with their hands.

Most of the hands I see have mixed fingertips, meaning some are rounded, some are pointed and some are square or spatulate. The Jupiter and Mercury tips are usually rounded, and the two middle fingers are either square or spatulate. I rarely see pointed tips on Saturn or Apollo, unless the Mercury and Jupiter fingertips are also pointed. I do see pointed Jupiter fingertips with mixed Saturn, Apollo and Mercury tips. I read this as someone who is intuitive and depending on the rest of their hand, make emotional decisions when people are involved but they are practical in matters of money and business.

Finger Pads

At the tips of each finger is a fleshy pad. A large bulbous pad high up on the thumb indicates a temper. This same pad a little lower on the thumb indicates a stubborn disposition. People can have tempers without the thumb being raised and fleshy, but this would be learned behavior and not genetic behavior. Violence when angry is also learned behavior and not genetic.

Tear drop pads on the other fingertips indicate sensitivity. Flat finger pads belong to someone who holds things inside.

Rings on the Fingers

When we buy a ring we choose it because it fits certain parameters. We like the way it looks, it fits our budget and it fits the finger we choose to wear it on. The choice of which finger you wear your rings on is directed by the unconscious. The ring just seems to be made for one finger. You are subconsciously making the finger stand out by wearing a ring on it and this references certain character traits you either possess or wish to strengthen.

When you wear your rings on the Jupiter finger, you are able to assume command of whatever situation you find yourself in. It means taking control of your life.

If you wear your rings on the Saturn finger, you are searching for your pathway to the spiritual world. This means you are searching for your own individual pathway.

If Apollo is the finger you choose to wear your ring on you are into design and color. You seek more color in your life when you wear more than one ring on this finger. This is called the ring finger and it is usually where you wear your wedding ring, as Apollo is also about your home; the home that you make for yourself.

When you put a ring on Mercury you show that you are confident with your communication skills.

If you wear rings on the thumb, you are unconventional and march to a different drummer than most people.

So, if you are insecure about your ability to be in charge of your life or a situation you find yourself in, put a ring on the Jupiter. Put two on just for extra oomph.

Whatever you feel insecure about, add a ring to the finger that covers that area.

Or you can be like me, and wear rings on all your fingers and on your thumbs.

CHAPTER 4

MAP OF THE HAND

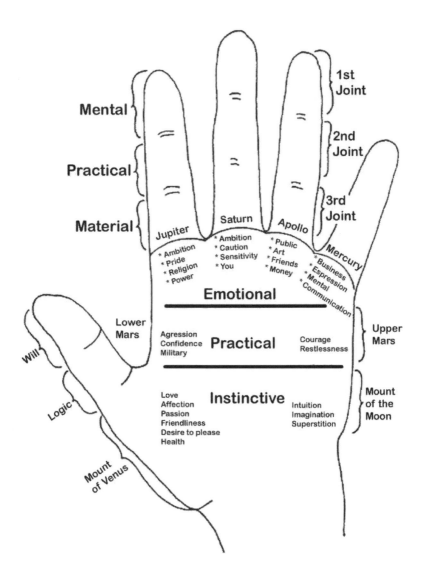

Map of the Hand

This is the Map of the Hand. Study this thoroughly and carefully. Memorize it. This map shows the names of the fingers, the pads under them and what they represent, the mounts and the different zones. The palm is divided into three horizontal areas which are named the emotional, the practical and the instinctive. On the left, between the thumb and the forefinger, is the area that is called Lower Mars and on the right, under the little finger, is the area that is called Upper Mars. In between this area is the Plane of Mars. Each area of the palm tells us more about the person we are reading.

Mounts in the Hands

Below each finger is a raised fleshy area called a mount. Each mount is named for the finger above it. So the mount under or near the Jupiter finger is called the Mount of Jupiter and so on. We are looking for a slightly raised pad. Excessive pads would accent the negative qualities of the finger.

Mount of Jupiter

A raised Jupiter Mount indicates the potential to be in a position of authority. It shows a strong sense of family and of society. It also shows self-respect and pride. If it is excessive, it indicates a tendency to go on an ego trip. It indicates conceit and haughtiness.

A flat mount would be someone who doesn't put themselves forward. They often have an inferiority complex. They are less likely to attain a leadership position. There are other places to find management in the hand, so if you don't have a raised Mount of Jupiter, don't worry, it doesn't condemn you to a menial position all of your life.

If the Jupiter finger is long and thick and the mount highly developed, it belongs to a person who is frequently religious and derives great comfort from the pageantry and show of church worship. But this doesn't always mean that a person will go into religion. I have a client who is a clothing designer and her well-developed Jupiter finger and high Jupiter Mount leads her to participate in pageants and parades with her clothing. She frequently sponsors, designs and builds intricate floats for themed parades. She is also well known for her ability to stay in front of the trends of the day. These people are 'up' for adventure. They have very little fear and seldom have negative thoughts about themselves or others.

Mount of Saturn

When the Saturn Mount is well developed it means a solitary person. If it is extremely developed it is someone who is fearful and somewhat morbid. This person is a serious, thoughtful person who is usually good with money. You would caution someone with a well-developed Saturn Mount and a long Saturn finger to lighten up, as they are often very self-critical. It is an OK trait to double check or second guess yourself, but too much inner criticism will stop a talented person from developing their talents.

Mount of Apollo

A well-developed Mount of Apollo gives the person the quality of mercy and a love for beauty and art. It gives them a desire for fame. This person is usually happy, quite emotional and never cruel. It is also someone who is very intuitive.

If the mount is in excess it can bring vanity, ostentation and a love of money. This person may have to watch that they don't become cruel.

Mount of Mercury

A well-developed Mount of Mercury gives the person a buoyant and happy spirit. It is someone who has hope, wit, merriment and great recuperative ability. This is someone who is gifted with an easy flow of words. If the palm shows a lot of intuition, then this person will know exactly what to say to people to influence them to do what they want them to do. This person can rise above troubles and emotional pain. They make light of their ailments.

If the mount is very high, it can mean someone who is manipulative and may stretch the truth. It is important for this person to have integrity, as when misused, this type of person can be involved in scams.

If the Mount of Mercury is very flat it leaves the person with no sense of humor.

Occasionally you will see a person whose Apollo mount drifts to the next finger and this leaves no room for the Mercury mount. Or you will see the Apollo mount and the Mercury mount run together. This usually means that these people make music with their voice. It doesn't always mean music as in singing. It can mean a wonderful speaking voice, a voice that sounds wonderful on the radio or in a recording.

Mount of Venus

The pad at the base of the thumb is called the Mount of Venus. This mount indicates both the vitality and the general health of the client. A well-developed Mount of Venus is someone who is generous, warm hearted and has an outgoing, lively personality. They have a lust for life and the energy to make life happen for them.

If the mount is too large you have someone who may dabble in extremes. They may drink too much, or eat too much. They are sometimes larger than life and their health may pay a price. Some of my clients with large, overdeveloped Mounts of Venus don't pay attention to their own body signals. They may work too hard as well as play too hard. Some of the men lift too much or don't take precautions when they lift, thus straining their bodies. I always caution these clients to pay more attention to what their bodies are telling them. Learn to stop.

If the Mount of Venus is flat, this is someone who isn't always able to share their emotions with others. It is someone who may not like to eat or remember to eat. They can also become aesthetics; they can shut out the world.

When the edge of the palm under the Mount of Venus seems to square itself off, it is called the Angle of Tempo. This person is often interested in music and will often play an instrument. Years ago, this person would have learned to play by ear, but today this doesn't happen very often as there are not as many people who sit around and play music together. But I have many clients with rounded palms who are also dedicated and fine musicians. The Angle of Tempo also indicates artistic leanings and these people are often involved in some type of art or craft.

Mount of Luna

The Mount of Luna is the raised mount that runs from under the Mercury finger to the bottom of the palm. If the mount is very well developed it shows tremendous imagination, creativity, and gives a love of beauty. It also shows empathy and a good memory. Tapping into Luna is tapping into the stored memories of your childhood and everything you have ever learned or dreamed about. Luna means lunacy and the moon. The moon signifies the unknown and magic.

A highly developed Mount of Luna belongs to someone who has the ability to tap into the fantastic and the mystical part of the brain. If the Head Line goes way down into this mount, it is the ability to tap into an unlimited imagination. The Head Line needs to be evaluated in its entirety to know what all this entails.

If the bottom part is highly developed, it is a person who needs a lot of physical energy to keep their mind clear. This is called the athlete's hand. These are naturally friendly people who like to do things with their hands. This is also an intuitive hand.

If the whole area is pretty flat, it is someone who is more easily discontented. This is someone who has less sympathy or empathy for others.

If the area is very high and the mount looks like it is spilling onto the wrist, you have a very eccentric person. They march to a different drummer and often 'see' things in an unusual way. When I say 'see' things, I mean both visually and mentally. They can see visions and this can be artistic visions, as well as psychic visions. They can see or sense ghost or spirit energy.

The Three Mounts of Mars

If you look at the Map of the Hand, you will see a rectangle through the middle of the hand. This is the Upper and Lower Mount of Mars with the area in between being called the Plain of Mars. The Upper Mount of Mars is under Jupiter and above the Mount of Venus.

A well-developed Mount of Upper Mars is called, the Warriors Mark. This is someone with bravery and courage and they never give up. They will physically fight for what they believe in.

A flat Mount of Upper Mars is someone who will still fight for what they believe in, but they may avoid direct confrontation. They may write a letter of complaint, or they may use the telephone to complain.

A raised Mount of Lower Mars is someone with great stamina. If the mount seems to slide off the hand, there may be too much emotion, depending on the Head and Heart Line. The Plain of Mars is rarely raised. When it is raised it is said to be a weakness in the system, but frankly, I don't recall seeing this area raised. If you do see a raised Plain of Mars, examine all the other lines and mounts, and if the other areas are strong, you would ignore this and not include this in the reading. If the other areas show weaknesses, you would caution your client to stop and think before they speak when they are angry. Or you would tell them to practice controlling their anger, and to speak softly in arguments.

If the top part of the Mount of Mars is highly developed or raised above the rest of the hand when you look at it sideways, this person is in tune with their emotions. But they can be ultra-sympathetic to other people. You would see this in a person who helps other people sort out their lives. They use their sympathetic and intuitive natures to help others. However, if they put every else's needs before their own, and work themselves ragged they aren't helping anyone, and need to watch that they don't get taken advantage of.

When the outside edge of the hand is curved, this is a very creative person. A straight outside edge belongs to a more logical person.

When there is a bulge on the outside edge of the hand, this person needs adventure in their life. This is an adrenalin junky. I point out to these people that they need to have challenges in their lives. It doesn't matter whether it is in business, athletics or buying and selling stocks, they need to have a passion that challenges them. The more difficult the challenge, the happier they are.

The Plain of Mars is usually in the practical section of the hands, but part of it will spill into the emotional section so keep this in mind when you interpret this area.

CHAPTER 5
MAJOR LINES OF THE HAND

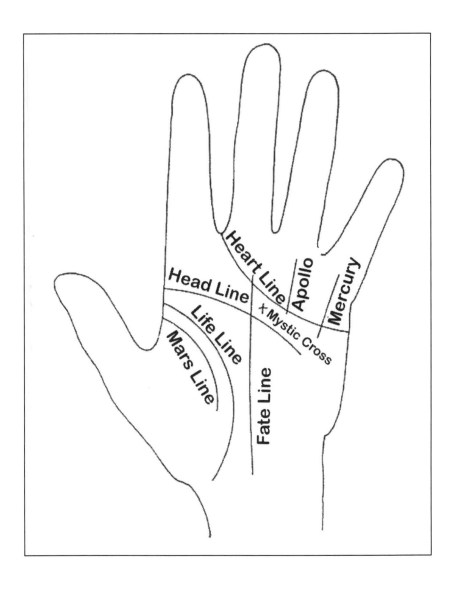

I don't try to compute time or age in the hand. Many books on palmistry divide the Life Line into segments and read time this way. They interpret breaks in the Life Line as a time when someone could have died from an accident or illness, but didn't. The reader will then say that the life continues, but they may get ill again at another break, or chained area. I haven't found this to be true. I do predict time when I do readings, but I do this with my intuition and not from the hands. I will explain how I do this in the chapters on psychic intuition.

People with deep lines have strong feelings. People with only a few lines on the hand have tremendous physical energy. Many lines show a nervous disposition. These people have energy and stamina but it comes from the mind rather than the body. This is an example of mind over matter.

Wavering, wriggling lines can indicate a rundown condition. Twisted, islanded lines indicate the person's hardest struggles come from within themselves.

Weak lines on a strong hand dissipate energy. Strong lines on a weak hand increase energy.

The major lines do change, but over a period of many years. The minor lines can change overnight, and I have seen them change during a reading.

Line of Mars-Guardian Angel Line

I begin the reading with the Line of Mars. I call this the Guardian Angel Line. We all have Guardian Angels. If you don't have a Guardian Angel Line, it doesn't mean that you don't have a Guardian Angel. I believe we all do and that they are assigned to us when we are born. The Guardian Angel Line is a nice line to have as it gives you the ability to network support when you need it. This doesn't give you a life without problems, but it does give you people to help you when needed. The absence of this line means that you may have to deal with your problems by yourself.

The Line of Mars or the Guardian Line is also called the Influence Line. It usually means that you have people that you have patterned yourself after at different times in your life. This can be parents, grandparents or other people you have admired and, whether consciously or unconsciously, have emulated them.

This line rarely doubles, but if it does I tell my client that they have extra strength right now. This strength can come from family or a feeling of support from God. This extra line is also called the antibody line and signifies good health.

Life Line

The Life Line is next. There are different opinions on where the Life Line begins and where it ends. I read the Life Line as beginning at the wrist but other palmists read it as beginning over the thumb. The Life Line shows your energy, your basic vitality and the way you embrace life, but it doesn't show the length of your life. This is in the bracelets on the wrist right under the palm, called Rachettes, and I choose not to learn to read them. If you are supposed to know the length of your life, God will tell you. People tell me that being forewarned is being forearmed. In this case that isn't true. If most of us knew the time of our death we would stop growing as a person. A reader shouldn't, whether amateur or professional, predict death. Most readers are unable to, even if they think they can. I have done shows where someone has come up to me and said, "Reader So and so--- said I was going to die last year so I cancelled all of my magazine subscriptions." And I tell them, "You shouldn't give anyone, including your reader that kind of power, and since you didn't die; perhaps you should go and deck them." This is facetious, but I believe that if a reader says that you are going to die, you should end the reading immediately.

The old lore is that a broken Life Line means accidents, illness or death at the time of the break. I haven't seen that this is true. I have studied the palms for over 40 years and I find people with intact Life Lines die young just as often as not, and some very old people have half a Life Line. I believe the breaks indicate change, moves and major life opportunities; but not death or illness.

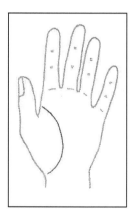

If your Life Line is centered in your hand, as in this picture, you have a nice flow of energy in your body. You are outgoing and balanced. You have intelligence and the ability to make good decisions. Your mind and body are balanced.

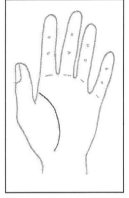

If it is broken at the wrist you can expect to move a long distance from the place of your birth. This may not be literal. It can be that you have grown and changed a lot since your youth and will continue to grow and change all of your life. You are moving mentally.

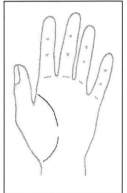

If it is open closer to the center, you can expect to move and come back to your place of birth. Again, this can be a physical move or it can be a mental move. You could be raised very conservatively, then have broken away and become a liberal. If you have the break in the Life Line close to the center, you go back to being conservative when you are older. Not everyone who has that break will do this so dramatically. The rest of the hand will moderate the distance you would move.

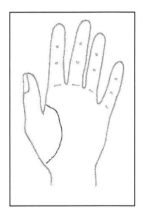

If the Life Line runs closer to your thumb, you are a very shy person; you may feel limited and restricted. It is hard to embrace change.

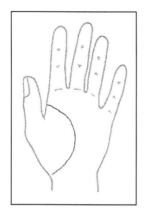

When the Life Line runs way out to-wards the center of the hand, you may take unusual risks with your life. I always caution people with this Life Line to take their risks in safe ways. For instance, if you enjoy driving fast, then race cars on a track instead of on the freeway. Climb mountains instead of drinking too much. You do need an element of risk in your life or you will feel unfulfilled. So join the police department, become an athlete or take risks in your career.

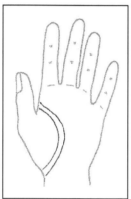

When you have a double Life Line you have versatility and stamina. It often means you begin life in one place and end up in a totally differ-ent place. This can be physically, mentally or emotionally. You can be born in one country and end your life in another country.

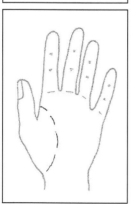

If your Life Line has many breaks you jump from job to job. When that pattern in your life is over, the breaks will fill themselves in. You may feel your life goes fast for a time and then slows to a crawl. Breaks in the Life Line mean that things in your life change, often it is a career change, but it can be physical moves as well.

However, one of my older clients had several breaks in her Life Line; she had moved less than two hundred miles when she was eight and a mile when she married at nineteen. She was a high energy person, had nine healthy children, and except for gall bladder surgery and a fall, she didn't have life threatening events in her life. She lived to be a hundred and one years. So, what does her broken Life Line tell about her life? It didn't start and stop; she didn't move a lot in her life; and she didn't have life threatening events. I read her as someone who had a great capacity for change; she didn't change her home, but she embraced change. It was emotionally easy for her to hop in a Model T and take a cross country trip, or take a Greyhound bus across the country, even when her life had started in the horse and buggy days. When plane travel came in she was excited to travel by plane and often did. I knew this woman well because she was my grandmother. Studying your family's hands is a good way to see how the lines have shaped a person's life, or how a person's life has shaped their lines. Not every break or mark on the lines means the same thing for each person. You must become very familiar with all the lines and where they sit on the hand. Then, when reading an older person, ask them questions, and check their lives with the meanings you know and adjust your knowledge.

Head Line

The Head Line begins at, or above, the Life Line and continues across, or down the hand towards the Mount of Luna. It needs to be examined for length and depth. It reveals the scope of your mental interests, your independence of thought and your creativity.

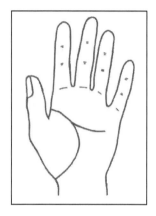

When you have a close connection at the beginning of the Head Line and the Life Line, you are skeptical and you don't believe things until you know them to be true. You are a rebel of sorts, and you think outside the envelope. You are your own person. You are verbally very skilled and can usually talk people into doing things your way. Making changes is pretty easy for you.

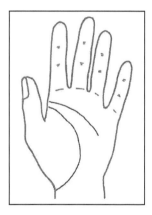

A wide split means that you don't care to be told what to do. You tend to procrastinate, and need to give yourself a shove to get started. You tend to become a hermit when things become difficult. You have trouble letting go of things that bother you. You don't embrace change easily.

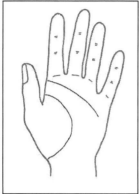

If the split is very wide, with the Head Line beginning on the Mount of Jupiter, you do need to set your goals down on paper. You get great ideas, but you forget them. Sometimes visually focusing on your goals helps you get started. You have tremendous creativity but lack action.

A very wide split between the Head Line and the Life Line on a teenager is someone who becomes 'snotty' or scornful when talking to authority. Adults get angry with them and they don't always know why. I point this out and tell these kids to speak in a soft voice, moderate their tone of voice and they will have an easier time.

A clear deep Head Line shows the ability to concentrate; you have a sound memory and a sharp mind.

Occasionally I will read for a person who has a close connection between the Life Line and the Head Line on one hand and a wide split between the Head Line and the Life Line on the other hand. These people have the ability to see many options. This can be useful, as they can help friends and family who are stuck. With a little thought about a problem, these people can think of many ways to solve the problem. They are lucky in that they see things from a different perspective and their ability to problem solve is unique. They are able to focus on more than one thing and they multitask easily. However, when it comes to making decisions about their own lives, they get too many ideas and can't decide what they should do. They give themselves too many choices. I advise this client to say out loud, "I will know what to do at the moment." If they do this every day, it helps them make decisions intuitively, and they stop weighing and balancing everything. Their multi-tasking can get away from them and they can have too many projects going at the same time. One way to fix this is to prioritize. To do this I recommend that they put all their projects into columns marked A, B, or C. Put each project into one of these columns, depending on its importance and don't do the C's. Do the A's daily, the B's if you have time and leave the C's. Sometimes it is not important for them, or anyone, to finish all their projects. The act of starting a project may be all that is needed. They need to quit beating up on themselves.

A Head Line that slopes slightly to the Mount of Luna is

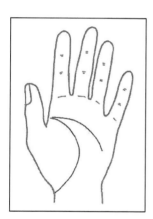

called the 'writer's curve'. It is an access into the right brain, or the imagination and most writers have this. It doesn't mean that your client will be, or desires to be a writer; it means they access their imagination and they really can't handle mental boredom. This person needs to keep their mind busy, or they can become depressed. A very gradual slope is creativity based in the rational mind.

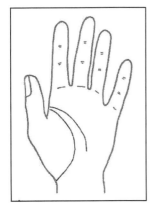

This is also a writer's curve but notice how the Head Line parallels the Life Line. This exaggerated curve is every bit as creative, perhaps more so, but this person needs to control their fantasy life and they need discipline to be productive. Whether their talents lie in art, business or personal relations, they are creative, but they have trouble focusing. This person has a touch of attention deficit disorder.

Both lines have a tendency to need to be busy or they get depressed. They cannot handle boredom. This doesn't mean housework or lawn work, it means challenging the mind with plans, classes, and projects that help stretch the mind.

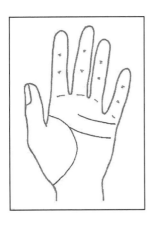

The straight Head Line cuts the hand in half. This is also called the Sidney Line. The person who has this line can see right through people. They see the games that people play and their inner motivation. They need to surround themselves with people who don't play games. This line is a management tool. People who have this line are good managers.

A straight Head Line that doesn't cut the hand in half is a logical Head Line. These people have spatial orientation, good reasoning skills and math skills. They access the left brain or the logical brain.

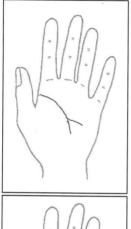

Occasionally you will see a Head Line that forks into the instinctive and practical parts of the hand. These people are very versatile and are able to communicate with everyone. They don't trust their creativity as much as they could because the practical side dominates. It is easier for them when they learn this about themselves.

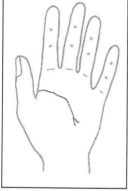

If the fork is short, it is called the lawyer's fork. It looks like a forked tongue and that is why it was named the lawyer's fork. This is good argumentation skills as well as the ability to see both sides of an issue.

Some people have a logical Head Line on one hand and a creative Head Line on the other hand. This is read as someone who can access both the practical, left brain and the instinctive, right brain. It is a good thing to access both sides of the brain, because it gives them the ability to see both sides of an issue, but it is important to point out to your client that they need to learn to trust the creative side of their system as their logical side will try to dominate.

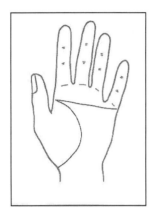

Simian Line

This shows the Head Line and the Heart Line going together to form one line across the palm. It looks much like the Sidney line but without the Heart Line. It is called the Simian line and it is a rare line. All races have this line, but it is slightly more common in Asians. The people who have this line are very intense. They can be very one faceted and have tunnel vision. It is difficult for them if they put that single minded energy into a relationship. If the other person doesn't feel the same way they do, the Simian line person has a hard time changing their focus. This type of person is happier putting their tunnel vision into a career focus and not into a relationship. In business it is often a very successful person, one who sees their goals and not the obstacles.

The intense feelings that their system generates can bring on mood swings and this is helped if they are very physical. Exercise releases chemicals in the brain that help them relax. The Simian line got its name from a long ago palmist in England who decided it looked like a monkey's palm. I have looked at the palms of apes and monkeys at different zoos and I can't see the resemblance, but the name has stuck.

The Simian line is hereditary, and so if you have it, one of your parents or grandparents have it, and you will pass it on to your children or grandchildren.

This line has been very misunderstood in the Western World. I read for a woman who has Simian lines on both hands. She told me that the doctor who delivered her told her parents that she was retarded and should be institutionalized. This was many years ago when the retarded were often institutionalized at birth. Her parents refused, but I shudder to think of the consequences to her if they hadn't.

A young boy told me in science class his teacher had all the kids show their hands. He has Simian lines on both hands and the teacher told the class that he would be a criminal and end up in jail. In fact he is now an engineer and a very successful person.

I reassured both of them that this doesn't indicate mental retardation, nor does it indicate criminal activity. These lines show intense energy, which can be used positively or negatively. I read for very successful people with the Simian lines and also for people with so many issues in their lives that success eludes them.

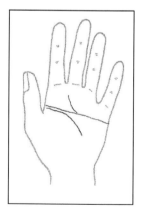

Today I see more people with Simian lines on only one hand, or a modified version, where the lines go together, but the person still has a Head Line and a Heart Line. In this case, I read the Heart Line and the Head Line and then talk about how such an intense focus can be good or it can get in their way. I add the meanings of the Simian line to their reading.

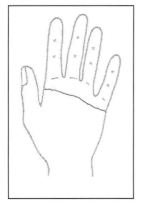

When the Heart Line and the Head Line go together to form one line that is in the Heart Line position, it is a called the Heart Simian. This is someone who wears their heart on their sleeve and their feelings get hurt easily. They need to develop some armor against that. They also lead with their emotions. They make decisions based on emotions and how they feel about a situation, which isn't necessarily bad, especially if they are intuitive. They are often people who focus on relationships with all their hearts and have trouble letting go if the relationship doesn't work out. These people put blinders on and see only what they want to see. This is intense and if the person they focus their love on doesn't love them in return, it is hard for them to let go and find someone else. This goes for friendships and careers, as well as love relationships.

Both the Head Line and the Heart Line Simian hands have a tough time being flexible. When the fingers are flexible, it gives the person an ability to make changes easier. It also helps them to hear that these are physical, human lines and these characteristics can be changed.

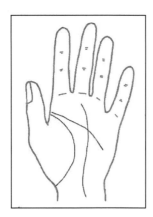

Fate Line

The Fate Line is like the rudder of a boat: when the rudder moves, the boat changes course. To read the Fate Line correctly you need to find where it starts and where it ends. The wrist or the wrist area is the beginning area of the Fate Line and the end is somewhere in the upper part of the hand.

Most Fate Lines do not run the entire length of the hand, but if it does, as in this example, this is a person who isn't swayed by other people's opinion. They set a goal and they meet that goal. They stay focused on the bottom line. But, if the Fate Line is very deep, it often means the opposite. The person's energy is supposed to go directly from an idea to completion, but the intensity of the energy itself may stop people. Sometimes they don't become successful until after middle age. The intensity of the line can send the person into a mental spin. They stop and start projects and change their direction a lot when they are young.

This may seem impossible to grasp when you are learning to read palms, but over time you will be able to sense when the line is too intense for the person to handle.

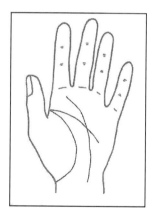

When the Fate Line ends deep in the Mount of Jupiter, it is a career in the public eye. It could be in theater, teaching, sales, management, fund raising or politics. It means visibility and the ability to motivate people.

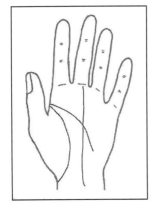

The Fate Line, ending deep on the Mount of Saturn means spirituality and the tendency to be introspective. If it feathers at the top, it is also a tendency towards melancholy or depression. The person who has this line without the feather can be successful in whatever he does. With the feather, the person needs to practice positive thinking and they can overcome the tendency towards depression.

If the Fate Line ends between Saturn and Apollo you will usually work in the technical aspects of the arts. This can include computer programming, writing and engineering.

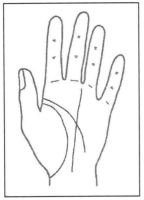

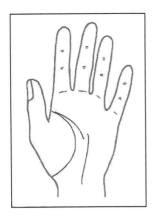

This shows the Fate Line ending midway up the palm. There you find your true vocation later in life. You may start several careers and find the final one in your mid-thirties.

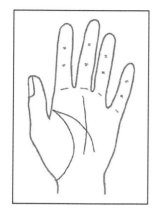

If your Fate Line begins in the middle of your palm, between the Mount of Venus and the Mount of Luna, you have an excellent balance between giving and taking in relationships and you handle people well.

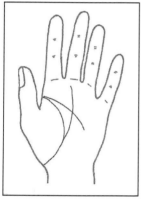

When the Fate Line begins in the Life Line, you follow a life plan that has been set for you by family, school or early life experience. You are a very independent person and you are often very sure of yourself but you have a hard time breaking away from other people's expectations easily. Sometimes you don't see a need to break away, either.

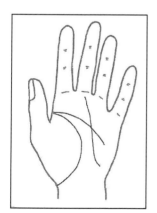

This shows your Fate Line ending on the Mount of Saturn. You often go into a helping or service profession. You call on your own intuition to help you through life.

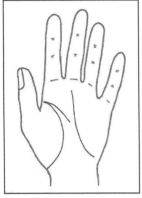

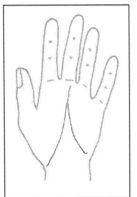

If your Fate Line begins deep in the Mount of Luna, you have ability in the psychic realm and you are very spiritual. This means your ideas come out of your imagination. It is also read as a self-made person, one who pulls themselves up by their boot straps.

A double Fate Line is usually seen as one that begins around the Life Line, wrist juncture and goes toward the Saturn finger. Then a second Fate Line will begin in the Mount of Luna and either meet, or run parallel to the first Fate Line. It means that you begin life doing what you think you should do, and at this time in your life you are deciding to follow your own pathway. This can mean going from a career to owning your own business. It can mean changing your pathway spiritually. It is finding your own way in life, not as other people see you but as you see yourself. Remember, not all lines mean physical events. They can mean inner or mental events.

Heart Line

The Heart Line begins above the Mount of Luna and ends in the center of the palm. It doesn't tell you about your love life, but it tells about your emotions and how you express them.

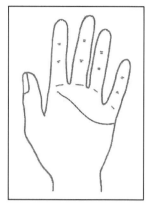

When the Heart Line ends on the Mount of Jupiter, it means that you are fussy and discriminating when choosing friends and lovers. You seek to marry well and are very loyal. You often have a strong voice and are able to project your voice across a room.

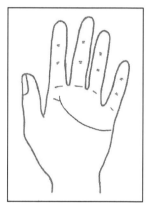

This shows the Heart Line ending with a fork on the Mount of Jupiter. This means you are lovable and loyal. You are fun to be with and you make a good marriage partner.

When your Heart Line ends on the Mount of Saturn you are idealistic and a perfectionist. You are hardest on yourself. You tend to see friends and lovers idealistically. You see them not as they are, but as you would like them to be. This leads to disappointment. You are an intuitive person.

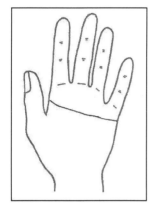

A Heart Line that runs across the hand shows you have a more rigid view of love. You put your loved one on a pedestal and God forbid they do anything to knock themselves off that pedestal. While you don't shower displays of affection on the person you love, you need your loved one to be focused on you.

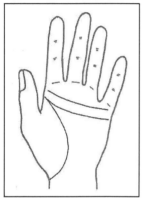

This shows the Heart Line cutting the hand in half, combined with the Sidney line which also cuts the hand in half. This is a person who tends to see issues in black and white. You come unglued when confronted with unexpected change and you tend to be nervous and high strung.

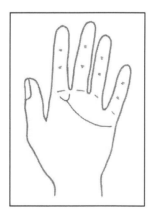

This shows the Heart Line ending near the Mount of Jupiter, with a fork branching off towards the Mount of Jupiter. This is a balanced person with a sarcastic sense of humor. This is someone who is loyal to their family and their friends. If the branch is long, then this person becomes a caretaker. This is someone who puts other people's needs before their own.

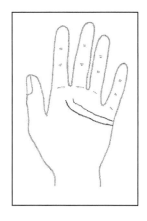

A double Heart Line is rare. When you do see it, examine it carefully to see where it begins and where it ends. If it begins under the Mercury finger and above the normal Heart Line, this adds emotion to the person's communication ability. It can mean that the person chokes up when they are in a speaking situation, especially when their emotions are involved. I tell this person that they need to practice what they are going to say before they speak so they don't get tongue tied. This is a person who is pretty emotional, but unless the lines are really chained, it is not someone whose emotions are uncontrollable.

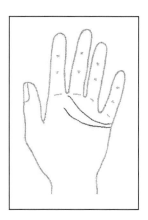

When the double Heart Line ends between the Saturn and Jupiter fingers and starts at the edge of the palm, it shows the tendency to cling to the people they admire or love. They may be possessive. If the double line is below the normal Heart Line, it is usually shorter than the normal Heart Line which gives the ability to bring a spark of passion to everything the person does.

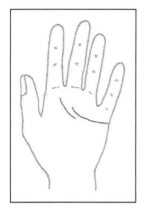

Usually the double Heart Line is read as a split Heart Line and this means a person feels separate or distant from their family. Some of the people with this split are adopted. Others have lost a parent at a young age to death or divorce. I reassure the person I am reading that I am not making a prediction when I say this. This would already have happened. The split Heart Line is something you are born with, and can create a feeling of distance in the person with this formation. Some people with this split move a long distance from their family, either physically or emotionally. The rest of the people with this line feel as if they are ducks and their family is chickens, or they feel as if they are ducks and the whole world is chickens. They feel as if they are a different species. Our lines are the tools we are born with. This tool, feeling different and outside of society, is often used by people who comment on society such as artists, writers, comedians and commentators. The feeling of being separate can be lonely, but if the person with this split makes a special effort to connect with people they will overcome this. If there is strength and length in the Mercury finger this person doesn't stay completely aloof.

Any other line that doubles would be read as strength. If any other line splits, it shows that the person with this split is in a time when additional strength is necessary.

Mystic Cross

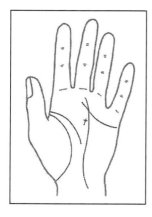

The Mystic Cross is in the center of the hand between the Head Line and the Heart Line. It can cross the Fate Line or sit beside it. This gives an indication of intuition or psychic ability. Intuition opens up as people evolve and grow spiritually. Almost everyone I read for has this line. I believe most of us have intuition, whether we acknowledge it or not. I feel that my clients pick me as a reader because something about me draws them to me.

Some mystic crosses are deep and some are faint. This will tell you if the person trusts their intuition or not. The deeper the line, the more the person uses and trusts their intuition.

Remember the lines are not read alone. They must be studied to see where they begin and end. Even before you finish this book, take what you have learned and do a reading for a friend. Some people have many contradictions between the shapes of their hand, the fingers and the lines. Some things will negate each other. Look at every hand that you can, memorize the lines, the mounts and their meanings. Put the meanings together and practice on every hand you see. It takes time to learn all the information that is in this book. It takes time to identify the lines in people's palms. It also takes time to recognize what you read and what you ignore in someone's palm. But if you memorize the line meanings

and practice finding them on the palms, you will soon be
reading palms as easily as reading a book.

CHAPTER 6

MINOR LINES
OF THE HAND

The Minor Lines

The minor lines are important to your understanding of the client's hand. Hands are full of lines, but not all of them show at any given time. For instance; if your hand has been in a cast for a few weeks, when the cast comes off you will see many more lines than you usually see. All these lines will show until you use your hands again and then some of the lines recede. I notice that some lines will appear during a reading. I believe the minor lines change as your thoughts change. The theory is that as you use your hands your brain sends electrical impulses through to your hands. You are thinking about your life while you are using your hands and the electrical impulses cause the minor lines to change.

The Apollo Line

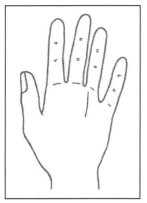

The Apollo Line runs upward under the finger of Apollo and may start from the Life Line, the Plain of Mars, the Mount of Luna, the Heart Line or the Head Line. Not everyone has this line and it can have varying lengths. The Apollo Line shows the extent that money matters occupy the mind, whether as anxiety over money matters or the acquisition or accumulation of wealth. This is also luck in money matters. It is someone with a good eye for color and design. It is said the sun shines on those who possess this line. Having this line gives the possibility of becoming wealthy.

If the line is clear and uncrossed it indicates that the person is free of care and worry at this time.

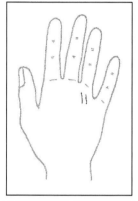

When there are two or more lines under the Apollo finger it means money will come from two different sources. Usually both are from earned income such as from two jobs or two businesses.

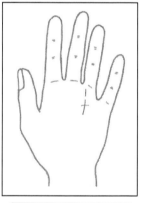

A broken Apollo Line or one with bars across the line shows loss of money.

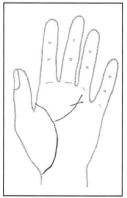

Lines rising from the Life Line and cutting through or breaking the Apollo Line are signs of money loss through loans you make to friends or relatives.

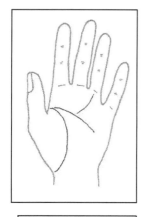

When the Apollo Line rises from the Head Line it indicates success later in life.

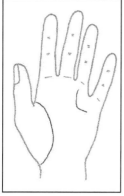

Lines from the Apollo Line show to some extent in what manner money has been earned. If the lines point towards Mercury it will be some type of business relating to communications.

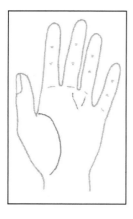

If the line points towards Saturn it is more likely to be from investments in land.

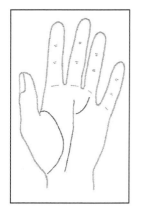

If the Apollo Line rises from the Fate Line it indicates business partnerships.

When the Apollo Line begins near the wrist and runs unbroken to the Apollo Mount it is supposed to be read as someone who sets a creative goal and never deviates, thus insuring great success. I find that this isn't true. It is almost as if the energy is too strong for the person with this, and they don't really ever start. They think a lot about what they want to do, but seem to shy away from actually doing anything with their ideas. If they do focus their creative ideas, it is usually as they get older.

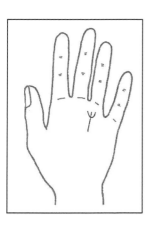

When there is a Trident under the Apollo finger you can achieve fame or the potential for recognition. It is read as creativity will out, or genius will out. If you have this mark your own system will push you to excellence. Some people use their creativity in their business or in their profession. This would give them recognition from their boss or their peers for doing a job well done. When someone uses their creativity in art, the Trident means fame. But this also depends on what age they begin to use their creativity and how much time they invest in it. Fame won't float by you with the Trident, it must be earned, but the Trident gives you the possibility of fame.

The Mercury Line

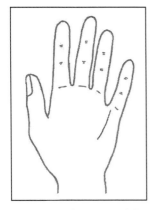

The line under the Mercury finger deals with communication. Some have a short line which gives the ability to communicate easily with people. Some have two lines that are very long. The double line indicates the possibility of speaking two or more languages. A lack of this line doesn't mean that you can't communicate with people; there are other areas of the hand that denote communication. It is just that people with the additional lines are more likely to work in a communication field.

Lines of Marriage and Children

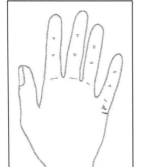

Most of the books about palmistry show the marriage lines beginning at the edge of the palm and running towards the Mercury Mount and they use the lines branching off the marriage lines as the children lines. The books explain that the lines may be affairs of the heart and not actual marriage lines. I find these lines do not match with what people actually do

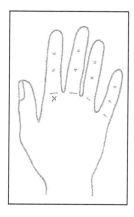

with their lives. If someone who is eighty years old has four marriage lines and has never even been married they probably haven't had four affairs either. I have asked my older clients what has happened in their love lives, and these lines have not matched with their life experiences. Therefore I do not use them in my readings. You don't want to be responsible for setting someone up for failure in their lives.

To find the marriage line, look for a large X on the Jupiter Mount. If there is one and the heart line is not deep red, their marriage should be good, or they will have a strong marriage in the future.

If they are single and not dating, I look at the Life Line. If there is a faint line moving from the life line to the Mount of Jupiter, and a small x on the Jupiter Mount, this means they will meet someone. This can be difficult for a beginning reader, as I also look at the space directly above their head and divide the area into twelve segments. If I see a sparkly area above the top of their head, I will predict that they will meet someone within the next six months. At times I see a picture in the hand, or in my mind, of what this person will look like. I tell my client what I see, but I ask them to take this with a grain of salt, as these visions can be tricky. They usually meet the person I describe but they don't always marry them. Sometimes they marry the person they meet right after the one I see in my vision. A strong X in the Jupiter Mount means that they will have a happy marriage in the future if they are single right now.

I find the children lines on the right hand, on the Life

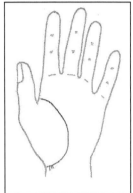

Line, where the wrist joins the palm. Having children is a choice that people make these days. They almost never have all of the children their hand will show. In a different day women married young and if they survived all of the pregnancies, they would have had all the children in their hands, but today that usually isn't so. I usually use the first two sets of lines to predict the number of children and this is the most accurate.

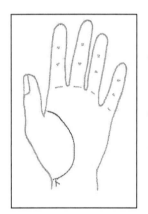

Two of the lines beginning together as a V indicate twins. Some books will say that this is either twins or babies less than eighteen months apart. A lot of my older clients, women who had children before the 60's when the pill went on the market, had babies less than eighteen months apart when they have this mark. Their children are adults, and I read for them and they have had twins. I am now reading for their grandchildren and sometimes they have the twins. So it shows the possibility of twins in the future. It can be twin children, twin grandchildren or great grandchildren.

If the line triples there is a possibility of triplets but this rarely happens.

Don't tell people they have four children waiting to be born, or three or any. Tell them the hand shows how many children they could have. Some people show eleven or even more. I read the first two sets of children lines as possibilities. If the first set shows two and the second three, I would say this indicates two to three or at the most five. But, I always tell people that if you have no children and don't want any that this is OK. If you don't have children and your hand shows children, I don't want to raise false hopes. If someone is childless, their hands show children, and they are of an age to have children; I tell them to go to the best fertility doctor they can find.

When people want to know what sex their children will be I will only predict this when they are actually pregnant. With ultra sounds they usually know the sex of their baby so they don't ask me to predict as often. I predict this psychically. I don't find the lines on the hands tell me the sex of their children.

If the Mount of Venus and the beginning of the life line are slightly swollen, the possibility of pregnancy is right now. There is also a slight discoloring in the very center of the palm, along with a small asterisk. The asterisk shows change in the body chemicals and it can indicate pregnancy.

Line of Intuition

Having the line of intuition in your palms is a mixed blessing. The line runs on the outer edge of the palm, running vertically from the Mount of Luna to the Mount of Mercury. It is shaped like an arc, arching out into the center of the palm. This is an acute, intuitive, understanding of life. It is an inherited type of psychic intuition that the person may or may not know they have. But it can leave a person feeling unsettled and they don't always realize that they are picking up energy from others.

If the person who has this line has weaker lines in the rest of the hand, they have a hard time telling their dreams from their reality. If this line is on a stronger hand it is intuition.

When I see this line I look at all the other strengths and weakness in the hands and the fingers. If the fingers are pointed and the hand is soft, I ask the person if they are bothered by visions or if they have noticed the ability to see ghosts or other entities. They usually have had some type of experience along these lines. I tell people to remember not to let this frighten them. They have the ability to control these experiences and if they do not like this ability, they can tell it to go away. I tell them to remember that we can choose to be open to our psychic ability or let it go. They need to get into a hobby that grounds them. Pottery, gardening, metal work, or anything of the earth will work.

Via Lascivia

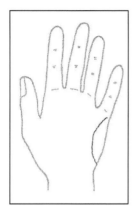

The Via Lascivia is a rare marking. It is a convex arch either crossing the hand above the wrist or slanting from the Mount of Mercury into the wrist. This line indicates intense physical energy. For this person life is more sensual and can be wonderful if the person doesn't over indulge in food, drink, work or anything.

Girdle of Venus

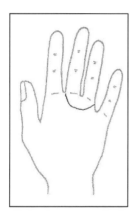

The Girdle of Venus is an arc looping down into the palm from between the first and second fingers and the third and fourth. Occasionally it stretches out from the Jupiter finger to the base of Mercury or even to the outer edge of the palm. It is a sister line to the Heart Line and if the Heart Line is absent it can take its place. People with a Girdle of Venus strive for the impossible.

If the hand is soft and there are a lot of lines and the Girdle of Venus is long, this is an overly sensitive person. They analyze everything. It is a good line for a person who is in a career where analyzing is important. But if the person begins to analyze everything it can lead to anxiety. This person has a hard time relaxing, their mind spins, and if they don't have something to worry about, they will worry about what might happen or what could happen. I tell these clients that they need to find some way to stop their conscious mind. They can recite a poem or sing a song, but it must be the same song or poem each time their mind spins with worry. They need to find some exercises to stop this. In the chapters on psychic development I will add the exercises I do to stop my mind from spinning

Ring of Solomon

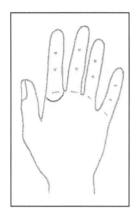

The Ring of Solomon is fairly unusual. It is a line that circles the Jupiter finger. It means the person has the ability to make sound decisions and often gravitates to a position in life where they are called upon to make decisions. I have seen it on judges, school principals and business leaders. It is also found on people who don't work and others who have jobs where they don't make any decisions. Thus, I read this line as someone who has the capability to make sound decisions, whether personal or professional.

Ring of Saturn

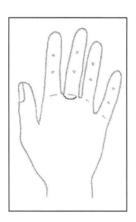

The Ring of Saturn is a line circling the base of the Saturn finger or it is formed of two lines starting on either side of that finger and crossing below it. This is someone who lacks constancy and I caution this client to write their goals down on paper and adhere to them. This is a challenging line, but it can be overcome.

Rachettes

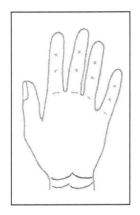

The bracelets are called the Rachettes. They are rings on the underside of the wrist, defining the lower edge of the palm. They may be absent or there may be one, two, or more. Most people have three Rachettes. Some of the older books say that each Rachette indicates thirty years of life, but I haven't found that to be true. I am blessed with clients who live a long time and relatives who live into their 90's and a few into their 100's. I notice that some have two Rachettes and some have a multitude of them. The Rachettes may indicate length of life in some way, but I choose not to learn to read them.

Lines of Travel

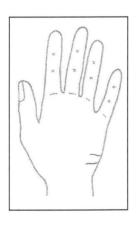

Lines of travel do not always predict travel. These lines indicate a type of restlessness which can include travel. This restlessness can drive the client to move or change jobs often or to travel frequently. I press my finger into the client's travel lines and the lines will darken if they are going to take a trip within the next six months.

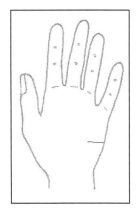

Immigration Line

A straight horizontal slash on the Mount of Luna is read as the immigration line. Today travel is so easy it is not always immigration. It can mean lots of foreign travel. Foreign travel can also be Hawaii or Alaska as they are not part of the contiguous United States.

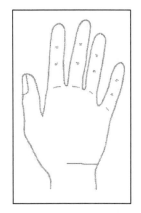

Poison Line

A horizontal slash that starts on the outside of the palm and continues across the Mount of Luna is called the Poison Line. This indicates that there is a high level of contamination in the client's body. Forty years ago I saw this only on people who had smoked for years or were really heavy drinkers. Today I see it on young people. I believe this is from all the chemicals in our lives. We have chemicals in our food, in our clothes, and in the air we breathe and the water we drink. This builds up in the body and it isn't good for us. If I see this line and it is really red, or a dark brown, it is someone who is using tobacco, drugs or too much alcohol. I bluntly tell them it is time to quit. The line may not go away for a long time but if they get rid of the chemicals they can control, the line recedes. Occasionally surgery and anesthetics will trigger the Poison Line.

I don't usually do health readings, but I do address the Poison Line. I will talk more about psychic development in the last chapters, but I have trained myself to see what is changeable in the hand. If I see something someone should or should not do, it is because they can change it. If it is unchangeable, I will not see it.

Chaining on any of the lines indicate weakness. They are usually found at the beginning of a line.

Chains on the Life Line indicate stress in the younger years.

Chains on the Head Line indicate trouble concentrating when young.

Chains on the Heart Line indicate a flirtatious nature.

A chain frequently circles the second joint of the thumb and it indicates an ability to argue their point of view.

CHAPTER 7

STARS, CROSSES AND CIRCLES....OH MY

Circles

Lines forming circles are fairly rare and can look oblong or round. Do not confuse these with the whorl circles.

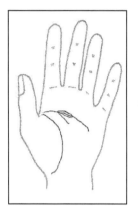

They are entirely different. I usually see circles on the Head Line or just under the Head Line and this means the person feels as if they are running in circles. They can't make headway. Just as they get something going, their life, fate or their own thinking seems to stop them. When I see this I look at the Life Line. If you see several lines going straight up from the Life Line, no matter how long they are, this indicates that the client will go forward again and make new choices. They will quit feeling like they are a gerbil running on a wheel.

If there are circles on the mounts this indicates success or honor in whatever they are doing.

A circle situated on the Mount of Luna indicates a dramatic imagination.

The circle under or near Saturn gives the person confidence, if it leans more towards Jupiter, there would be success in business endeavors.

The circle under, or near, Apollo bestows creativity.

A circle under the Apollo, leaning towards Mercury, indicates confidence and skill in creative vocalization. This can be singing, acting, sales, teaching and management.

It is important to see where the line or marking is situated in the hand. You need to see what mounts they are on or near, and where they seem to be reaching towards in order to interpret them accurately. At first this is difficult. It seems impossible to tell where a line begins and what line or mount it is reaching towards; it is hard to keep all these meanings in your head; but it will come to you with practice.

Crosses

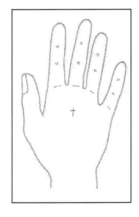

Crosses are often noted as negative but I don't read them that way. I find they have very diverse meanings depending on where they sit on the hand. The cross must be independent of the line. It isn't called a cross if it crosses another line. This would be called a dash and I explain these in the next chapter. A cross on the Mount of Jupiter, large and clear, or faint and receding, means marriage. If it is a cross high on the Mount of Jupiter it means ambition and success.

If the cross is on the Mount of Saturn it indicates that energy needs to be restructured. Perhaps the client needs to pay better attention to their health. Maybe better eating or more exercise. It can also be depression.

A cross under the Apollo finger gives keen observation.

A cross on the Mount of Mercury intensifies a strong business sense.

A cross on the tips of any finger gives special attributes, such as an aptitude for business if it is on Jupiter; religion when on Saturn; art when on Apollo and mysticism when on Mercury.

And of course between the Head and Heart Line this is the Mystic Cross. This is intuition and an interest in learning about the psychic arts.

Diamonds

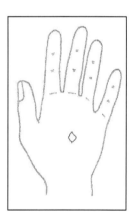

Diamonds are always money or success in a venture. Diamonds come and go in the palms.

If someone has a diamond on the Jupiter finger, it is a raise, bonus or some type of sale coming to them.

If it is on the Saturn finger it is inspiration.

On Apollo it is good luck.

On Mercury it can mean being on television or radio. I recall one time I was reading for a lady who was going to law school and I saw she would be on television. The next year she came back and told me she was in a class where they televised their presentations to help the budding lawyers see how they appeared to others. It wasn't television exactly, but they videotaped the presentation and it was shown on a television in the classroom. When the diamond showed up on my hand, I was interviewed on the radio for a show I was doing.

When I see an elongated diamond in the palm, I liken this to a sail on a boat. If it is wide, I tell the person that they are coming out of stagnant water or rough water and now they are hitting calm water. They will feel as if they are catching a favorable wind and reaching their goal easily. If the diamond is near the Life Line, it can be health or family issues. You don't need to identify the issues, just tell the client that they are solving the problems and it should get easier. If you can identify what the problems are, that is even better, but that would be done intuitively. The problems always relate to the area of the hand the elongated diamond is near. For instance, on the Heart Line it is a matter of relationships; on the Head Line it is school, money for school or it can be about business decisions. Look at the elongated diamond, identify where it is and you will know how to read it.

Recently I saw one diamond on the Mount of Venus, near the wrist, and another half way up the communication or Mercury lines. I read this as someone who was going to find a way to make a living with his passion or to find a way to develop a passion into a way to make a living. Then he would teach or sell this passion to the people he was trying to reach. When the reading was finished, my client told me that his passion was weight lifting and football. He wanted to teach and coach both, at community centers, schools and fitness centers. These diamonds showed that this was possible and he could turn this into a good business. He also had a small diamond on the Mount of Mercury and one near the Apollo Mount. This showed that he has the possibility to be on television or to be interviewed because of his accomplishments. He could also decide to make videos or write with the combination of his lines and the diamonds. I cautioned him that while he still had to work hard to be successful, the probability of success was high.

Grilles

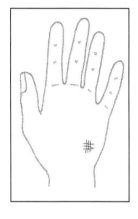

Grilles are made up of many lines crossing in opposite directions, resulting in a screen effect. I have noticed that grilles come and go-or they fade in and out. When a grille is very obvious and stands out one needs to pay special attention to this area of the palm and the other lines around it. It is a blocking energy so the client will feel blocked, but remind them it is temporary.

The Big M

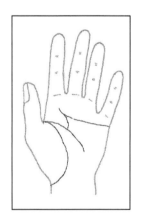

I can't tell you how many people ask me about the M in their hands. This is formed when the Head Line connects with the Heart Line and the Head Line also connects with the Life Line forming a large M in the palm. Most people have been told that means money. However, I point out that it would have to be a Pound sign for the English, an E for Euro or an R for Rupee and so on. I do think it can signify good fortune when this formation occurs, but one wouldn't spend money anticipating wealth with this formation.

Islands

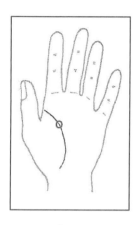

Islands appear on the lines in times of stress. Usually this stress is temporary. An island is read according to the line it is on, and the area of the palm it is on. For instance, if it is on the Heart Line, this indicates that this person was, or is, heartbroken. It could be current, trouble in the relationship they are in; or it could mean a recent past relationship. If they are overly sensitive people, it could mean they are stressed because of a slight or insult they had received. On the Life Line, it would be stress around job or home, on the Head Line it is stress in the thinking process. Usually if there is an island on the Heart Line there will be one on the Head Line as well. If there is an island on the Head Line and on the Life Line, the trouble would be around the job. It takes some time to get the feel of this, but persevere and it will come to you. Remember, islands indicate temporary problems. The stress will be resolved, sometimes without the client doing anything to solve it.

Stars

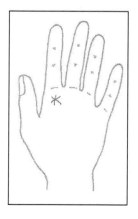

Stars are exciting to have anywhere. They can be on the fingers, the lines or the palms. They can actually be lines that form a star or they can look like asterisks. These denote sudden happenings.

A star or asterisk on the Jupiter Mount means that the person has the decision making ability and the drive to rise to the top of their position or to own their own business. They will have the courage to do this.

If it is on the Mount of Saturn, this is someone who is driven to live a spiritual lifestyle. This can be as simple as living a less cluttered life and embracing whole foods, or it can be as intense as giving up the world to enter a convent, monastery or ashram. But a weakness of finding a star here is that this person can have a problem with depression and that needs to be addressed.

On the Mount of Apollo, a star often means being recognized for something they are working on at the moment. This is an indication of wealth and position in life. If on Mercury, it means being on the radio or television. On either Apollo or Mercury, it indicates a prominent career. On the thumb pad it is learning a new skill and on the Mount of Luna, it is in designing or inventing. I do read for many artists and for them an asterisk on the Mount of Luna is often some type of artistic design. However, on a really logical hand, it can be inventions and people with this often have patents in their name, or will have if they trust their ideas enough to follow through with them.

If the asterisk is large and has a lot of sparkle I read that as the Spider Woman mark. Spider Woman is the Goddess of Creation in some Native Religions and She is credited with spinning the world into reality at the beginning of time. I read this as gathering all the thoughts and ideas one has and spinning a new reality for oneself, or spinning a new idea or concept. It can also be read literally and then this would be someone who becomes a seamstress or a weaver. It can also be a machinist or someone who follows blueprints.

A star on the tip of the Mercury finger indicates a facility for language and the person will have spell-binding charisma. They would be using some type of communication for the joy of doing it and if financial success comes with it, this is incidental. If it is on the middle phalange, it indicates the same gifts, but deliberately using them for financial gain. Thus you would want them to have a strong hand or this is someone who could mis-use these talents, especially if they are in careers where they wield influence over others.

Squares

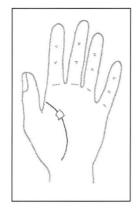

A square is usually a sign of healing. It binds the lines together and over-comes whatever line is broken. The square is read in relation to the posi-tion it appears. On the mounts it is protection and on the line it means preservation. The person you are reading for is over the problem and can go on with their lives. A square on the Heart Line is called a teacher's square and it is common on teachers but people can have a square without being a teacher. This person is patient, and usually finds a career that they love.

A square on the Mercury finger, down near the base, is someone who has a poker face. In this case it is some-one who can blend into any situation. You can see the advantage to have this on the communication finger in careers like law, undercover work for policemen, and gamblers.

Squares on the Life Line indicate strength. No matter where it is, it strengthens their life now. If the square is on the Life Line, the person's energy will get stronger, but a square doesn't indicate bad health. If the square is on the Head Line, it is a mending of the mind. On the heart it is read as emotional strength. I have not found that a square on the Heart Line indicates any physical heart issues. In fact, I don't usually read for health. If someone asks a question I am able to hear an answer, but this doesn't come from the hand.

A square inside the Life Line, on the Mount of Venus, means that the client feels stuck or they have just come out of a situation where they felt like they were in prison. This has meant an actual prison for a few of my clients, but usually, it is a prison of their own making. I look over their hands to find a strength that can help them to break the chains that keep them stuck.

Tripod

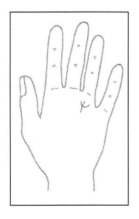

A tripod is a fork with two, short, even branches. This is recognition or fame where ever it lands. This is always someone who can make their mark on the world. However, they have to work at it. Fame won't float by you. You can't just reach out and grab it. It takes lots of work and then fame is awarded you.

Triangles

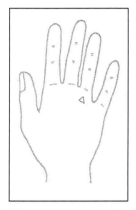

Triangles enhance the positive aspects of the area of the hand it is on. On the Mount of Jupiter it means that the person is inspired to rule a kingdom. Their kingdom can be their sports group, their family, their business, their community and so on. They are leaders and are often thrust into leadership roles.

When a triangle is formed between the Head Line and the Heart Line it is also called the trainer or teacher's mark. These people love to impart their knowledge to others.

On the Mount of Saturn the triangle counteracts much of the depression that other lines convey. If there is a triangle on the Mount of Saturn and a trident on the Mount of Apollo, the recognition the trident brings would have a very spiritual note. For instance, if the client was a writer, he or she would write a spiritual book. But don't jump to conclusions and think traditional religions when you see this. Being spiritual for some people means embracing the mythological, so you could see a person who writes about vampires and fairies with this mark.

If the triangle is on the Mercury Mount, it means success with communication. Some people tell me they communicate through their paintings and others through their sculptures. Communication can mean more than reaching others with words, so when you are reading hands don't lock into only one way to interpret this.

Triangles on the lines, near the lines, or in the other mounts mean issues improve. On the Head Line it means improved thinking or clearer ideas. If the triangle is on the Heart Line, it means a gift from someone. But remember, a gift can be an idea, or kind words, as well as a material gift. A triangle on the Mount of Luna is a stellar imagination. The people with this formation need to pay attention to their ideas. A triangle on the finger of Mercury is a diplomat. It is someone who is successful as a public speaker. A triangle on the finger of Apollo is someone who is a genius. On the finger of Saturn, it is someone who is a natural counselor. On Jupiter we are looking at a natural politician.

CHAPTER 8

LINES ON THE
LIFE LINE

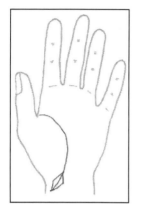

The lines and special marks on the Life Line need intense scrutiny. The Life Line begins at the wrist, and here you will often see a large triangle or diamond. Years ago this was read as farming or share cropping, or making a living off the land. This is still true, but it can be making a living with rental property, building houses, cleaning houses, a home office or any way that a person makes money out of their home. This mark can be there for years and nothing happens, but then it does and they will have some type of home office, or they are making a living off the land in some way. The opportunity will occur; but that doesn't mean they take it.

When there is a wide open space on the Life Line, at the base of the wrist, a move is indicated. If there is a straight line on the Mount of Luna this can be a long distance move or even a foreign move. This move would be within eighteen months and it will close up several months after the move has occurred.

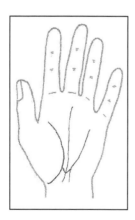

The lines at the base of the wrist, from the Mount of Venus to the Mount of Luna, will form into a faint W. I read this as they are ending one chapter in the book of their life and are now writing a new chapter. They are also writing their own words and not walking through someone else's script.

They are finding themselves. They are seeing themselves as who they are, and not who they are expected to be. They are making their own way in the world.

When these same lines form a butterfly at the base of the wrist, the client is making a transition from being closed off and they are moving into a time of feeling open to the excitement of life. This is a time of transformation. Sometimes this transformation is inner, within the person's thoughts, that later leads to changes in their lives. Other times this transformation is literally changes in their lives. But these changes are almost always for the better.

When the lines make a heart, the person is healing in the heart area of their life. Usually this is healing over a loss around people they love. It doesn't always mean a loss through death; it can mean the end of a relationship, or tremendous worry around a family member. It can also be a healing because someone has lost their job, or they are struggling in their business. It can be worry around health or friendship too. But it has already happened, it is not a prediction.

Just the other day, a lady I was reading for had the largest heart I have ever seen and she had recently lost both of her parents within ten days. The heart stretched way into the Mount of Luna. Her parents lived in a foreign country, and because of circumstances, she had not seen as much of them as she would have liked, so her grief was stretching very wide on the palm.

Another place to look for grief on the hand is the center of the palm. There will be an asterisk there and it looks like a wobbly asterisk. I don't predict or even bring up death in a reading. I speak instead, of a feeling of loss or transition. If they want to tell me what has occurred, then I will go into more detail. Years ago, when I saw this asterisk, I said to the young man I was reading, "Oh, your dad has just died." He said that this had not happened. The next week his mother came to me and told me his dad had died the next day. I realized then that you can't really tell the near future and the near past when you are doing a reading. There is an interval of about six months when you don't know for sure if something is coming or if it has happened. This is why I speak more vaguely of the grief and healing I see in the hand. Usually when you see grief in the hand it has already happened. Your body goes into shock when you hear of a death, or when you are fired from a job and this makes your body produce stress chemicals. This is what makes the hand change and forms the asterisk. Pregnancy can also make the asterisk appear as it's also a chemical change in the body. For pregnancy you would then look for a swollen feel on the Mount of Venus, where it connects to the wrist.

A cross between the Head Line and the Fate Line at the base of the palm indicates you may be called on to save someone's life. I noticed this formation in my hand for seven years and it wasn't happening, so I didn't use it in a reading. Then one day I saw someone having breathing troubles and I called 911. The person was having a heart attack and so calling an ambulance did save her life. To my amazement the line soon faded and was no longer noticeable on my palm.

A diamond on the Life Line means unexpected money. It usually sits at the middle of the Life Line and seems to have no relationship to the person's age. It means it has just happened or will happen in the coming year. In the past five years I have read for four people who have had friends or family win large amounts in the lottery and they have shared their winnings with my client. They had a diamond inside a square on the Life Line. If you have this formation, great, but I wouldn't wait for the money to come, as this is rare. Usually unexpected money has amounted to less than $90.00, although it has amounted to a lot more. I have not read for anyone who has won the lottery, but if you know of anyone who has, please have them send their hand prints to me with the date they won and their age. Once I see what this looks like, I can predict it for others.

Diamonds scattered over the hand, and especially more than one on the Life Line, is tremendous wealth.

Lines coming up from the Life Line, just under the Jupiter finger, denote job or business opportunities. When I touch this area of the hand I focus my eyes on the line, sort of cross my eyes, and if the job opportunity is coming, the line turns bright pink or gets darker.

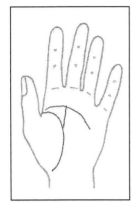

The buyer's eye is a line that comes up from the Life Line and touches the Head Line, forming a triangle. It is the ability to see trends. It is called the buyer's eye because buyers for department stores have this line. You will see it on artists, hair dressers, accountants and bankers. It can be used in any career where seeing trends can be helpful.

If you are in school you will know what to study, because after a few classes you know what information your teacher thinks important enough to test you on. You see the trends of the teacher.

CHAPTER 9

WHORLS, ARCHES, AND LOOPS

Each of our fingerprints has unique, individual patterns on them. Fingerprint identification is used to identify criminals who are careless enough to leave them at the scene of a crime. There are reams of study material on fingerprint technology, used mainly by law enforcement, but there are a few palmists who specialize in the fingerprints for their readings. The meanings I use are as follows.

Arches and Whorls on the Fingertips

Simple Arch

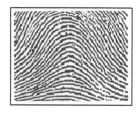 The simple arch belongs to a person who is less practical, but reliable, and unusually clever with their hands. This can indicate a natural artist. This person is good with others and generally fits in with people.

Some of the books that deal with the fingerprints say this is a lack of ambition, but I don't believe this to be true.

Tented Arch

 The tented arch is someone who is stubborn and doesn't give up on an idea, or a person. This can be an excellent quality, but they don't compromise well. These people can be somewhat impulsive. They have the ability to organize thoughts and information, and they complete their projects.

Radial Loop

An arch that slopes sideways is called the radial loop. People with radial loops are people who stand out and have inventive minds. They are easy going, and are good at finding compromises. Yet, there is an individual streak in this person as well; especially if you see this formation on all of the fingertips. They are dependable to a fault. This is someone who can shut out the world when they are focused on their passions.

It doesn't matter whether they have a left radial loop or a right radial loop in palm reading. It does for the fingerprint identification folks.

Whorl

The whorl looks like a bulls-eye with concentric rings around the center. You find these on people who are individualists. They like to have their finger in other people's pies, so if you don't want to share your life's ambitions, or your struggles, don't get involved with someone who has too many whorls on their prints. They are secretive, original, and usually highly motivated. They are usually their own boss, especially if both the thumb and Jupiter finger have a whorl on it. They aren't very people orientated, they are goal orientated. If someone has whorls on each finger and on the thumb they are a law unto themselves. They are extremely independent and very forceful.

Arches and Whorls on the Palm

There are arches and whorls in the palm itself. These can be a combination of loops, tented arches, simple arches and whorls.

There are times when there is more than one arch formation near each other in the palm, or on the finger, although this is more commonly found in the palm. Both will need to be examined to help you determine how to read this.

If someone has a radial arch and a tented arch near each other, it would bring the stubborn quality of the tented arch together with the creativity of the radial loop. This person would be very likely to keep plugging away until they found whatever success they desire. They would never give up on their creative dreams.

Mount of Venus

A simple arch on the Mount of Venus indicates determination. It is also someone who doesn't feel all the aches and pains of their body. It indicates strength of mind and of body.

A tented arch on the Mount of Venus is someone who is stubborn and usually focuses on what they want and goes after it. This is an inventive mind.

A radial arch that looks like a large loop on the Mount of Venus indicates courage. When it is closer to the thumb it means that the person will fight for what they believe in. It means the person is an individualist and very creative. This individual has the courage to be themselves, as well as the courage to stand up for what they think is right. This is someone you wouldn't want to cross.

A whorl on the Mount of Venus is an eccentric person. They are good at expressing themselves. If the whorl is found on a hand with a firm Mount of Venus, this is an athlete and if it is found on a hand with a soft Mount of Venus, this person is a romantic. Although that's not to say we can't have a person who is a romantic athlete or an athletic romantic.

Between the Fingers or On the Finger Mounts

It is unusual to see arches or whorls on the finger mounts, or between the fingers. When you do see them, you need to incorporate the meaning of the finger they are under into the meaning of the arch or whorl.

Jupiter Mount

For instance, any mark on the Jupiter Mount relates to the meaning of Jupiter. A simple arch on the Jupiter Mount means this person needs to be more practical. They are good with people, but they need to stand behind their words.

A tented arch on the Jupiter Mount would indicate a stubborn approach to their control issues. Jupiter indicates ambition, business, determination, and love of power, leadership and devoutness. This goes into relationships, career and physical energy. I would tell someone with the tented arch to be careful that they don't get so entrenched in seeking success that they get caught up in not seeing the forest for the trees, or not seeing the trees for the forest. They can err by getting caught up in seeing the big picture and jumping ahead of themselves, or they can get caught up in minutia and not achieve anything. Either way can change their potential for success to failure.

A radial arch is someone who may shut out the world and they do better if they are self-employed, or have a job that is very independent. They need to work for themselves as they don't delegate well. When they work with others they tend to take over and this irritates others. I tell this person not to isolate; but to include their co-workers in their decisions, and even further, to include their family and friends in their lives. Young kids with this often isolate themselves by getting lost in computer games.

A whorl on the Mount of Jupiter would mean great business, or financial success in whatever venture this person is involved with. This is not the same as a line circle, which is formed by the lines in the palm; this is a circle made by the skin patterns.

Between the Jupiter Finger and Saturn Finger

Any pattern between the Jupiter finger and the Saturn finger would include the meanings of Saturn. Saturn is you, your spirituality, your internal belief system, your faith, and the way you think.

A simple arch is someone who would counsel others to help them get past their problems. This person would mentor others.

A tented arch would be read as someone who is stubborn in their belief system and in how they do things. This faith in themselves can carry them past other people's criticism. But it can also shut out positive feedback from others as well. Sometimes self-doubt will make someone work harder and not rest on their laurels. I tell this person to keep striving for excellence in whatever they are doing, but to stop and get feedback from others on occasion.

Someone with a radial arch would have a tendency to shut out the world with spirituality instead of work. Spirituality can be any type of religion, or one's own belief in the universe.

A person with a whorl here would be someone who is a minister or works in a career that includes helping others. Depending on the rest of their hand, this can be a highly evolved person.

Saturn Mount

The whorls and arches on the Mount of Saturn aren't always as clear cut.

A simple arch on this mount is read as someone who is also good with people, but put other people before themselves. They can feel put upon after a time, so they need to set boundaries. When I see this in a reading, I tell them that no one feels their feelings, but themselves. If they put everyone before themselves, no one knows this. It is not selfish to put yourself first and to set limits on how much you will do for your job, your business or your family. The result will be someone who works to help others without resenting it.

A tented arch person has better boundaries. Selfishness describes the person who has this formation under the Saturn finger, but that is not all bad. Sometimes a strong self-interest is a saving grace, especially on a person who is very psychic and using it in a career where they help other people with their problems. This would give them naturally strong boundaries. You need to look at the whole hand to see how this arch affects a person's life.

A radial arch is someone who is very private with themselves and has better boundaries.

A whorl is someone who is usually into spirituality. This can be a traditional spirituality or non-traditional. This person can be an energy healer, or energy worker. These people are working on a higher level than most of us, but they often will suffer from melancholy, or depression. When I see this whorl, I tell my client to watch for signs of depression, as this is so fixable today. I will look for other signs in the hand that show depression before I read it as a fact.

Between the Saturn Finger and the Apollo Finger

When you see a simple arch between the Saturn finger and the Apollo finger, it is read as new confidence in the person's social skills. This also helps the person connect with people on a creative level.

A tented arch adds a stubborn quality to their belief in their own creativity. This can be good as the person never gives up on their creative ideas.

A radial arch is someone who has a unique vision to bring to their artistic skills. These are usually visual skills, as the person gets their ideas as visions, but people will write with this as well, getting their ideas visually.

A whorl brings the ability to utilize their ideas. The people with this are often geniuses.

On the Apollo Mount

Having any of the arches or the whorl on the Apollo Mount gives the person a less practical approach to their creativity. This is someone who is called an air head. They have their heads in the clouds and don't get as much done with their ideas. They need someone to hold the string of their balloon. They need grounding exercises. If they have a practical hand with sturdy lines this helps them use their creativity more effectively.

Between the Apollo Finger and the Mercury Finger

Arches and whorls in between the Apollo finger and the Mercury finger give extra creativity to the person's communication skills.

The simple arch is someone who is reliable, can speak in front of groups and is good with others.

A tented arch gives a firmer, more concise ability to communicate. These people don't pontificate. This is someone who is good with people and doesn't give up easily.

A radial arch is someone who often does motivational speaking and has a quirky sense of humor.

A whorl is someone who truly is gifted with words and has the faith in themselves to use this gift.

Mercury Mount

A simple arch under the finger of Mercury also shows excellent communication skills, but this person could be somewhat shy when their feelings are involved.

A tented arch is the determination to make a difference and they speak out about their beliefs.

A radial arch is an individual who is excellent in communication with others. This person writes well, speaks well and is comfortable in the public eye.

A whorl is someone who has a pretty singing or speaking voice. This is someone who finds recognition or fame for their communication skills. Again this can be writing as well as vocal. This person is often in the public eye in some way.

On the Mount of Luna

The only other place I see arches and whorls in the palm is on the Mount of Luna. However, nothing is absolute. If you see any type of arch or whorl anywhere else you will need to see where it is on the hand and incorporate the area meaning with the arch or whorl meaning.

When a simple arch is high up in the Mount of Luna, it is someone who has a more practical approach to their lives. They usually use all of their ideas in their jobs.

A tented arch brings determination to their approach.

A radial arch is someone who brings enthusiasm to their ideas.

Whorls are rare here but they do exist. This person is someone who thinks outside the box. They need to use their ideas in their own business. An employer would not always be able to accept the way they do things.

When the skin ridges on the Mount of Luna are very noticeable and they look as if someone has pulled a fine tooth comb through them, this is the engineer's hand. These people see structurally and often become architects, computer programmers, engineers, surgeons and accountants.

If the person also has the athlete's hand with the engineer's hand it gives them good timing. This is excellent to have in sports and careers that need good timing to survive or to win. They also have good eye to brain coordination, which makes them a good shot and a good golfer. In fact, they are usually good in any activity that uses these abilities.

I read for a gentleman who has an athlete's hand, along with the engineer's formation. He had a strong writers curve and a raised warrior's mark on a strong Mount of Venus. He had an unusually strong Apollo line and an asterisk on the Mount of Jupiter. His hand was strong and his lines were deep. This can often mean a professional athlete and he was in a particularly lucky time with the strength of the Apollo line. There were diamonds on the Mercury line and on the Mount of Apollo, between the Saturn and Mercury finger. I read that he was going to win whatever type of competition he was in; that he would win money and recognition as well as have his picture in the paper and be on television. He needed to keep his focus, not let himself get sidetracked, and he would be very successful. I told him that I thought he was a warrior with the heart of a poet.

It turned out that he was a professional football player and his team won the Super Bowl that year. When I saw him the next year I told him he would win again and his team did, indeed, win a second Super Bowl that year. I also told both he and his wife they had the possibility of having twins each time I read them. This went on for years and each time they assured me that wasn't going to happen. Last year, they came with their twin boys.

If there is any type of arch formation at the end of the Head Line, it gives the person the ability to come up with different ways to do things. Often people with this hold patents or will hold patents.

If a simple arch is at the end of the Head Line, it is someone who can invent, or can use their ideas to write and publish.

A tented arch is someone who doesn't give up on anything easily.

A radial arch is someone who doesn't compromise easily. This is someone who is an individual thinker, and when this person is excited about an idea they can shut out the world.

A circle whorl is someone who is a designer and someone who is eccentric.

People with the whorls are restless, and need to find their dreams and a way to honor their dreams. They need adventure, and are able to think way outside of the box. They need a certain creative freedom in their lives.

I have clients with this whorl who are huge clothing designers, others are leather workers and others are artists. I also have read for people with this whorl who are in traditional careers and they are happiest when they have exciting hobbies. These people are often outspoken.

CHAPTER 10

MYSTERY MARKS

Mystery marks are rare markings or lines that I see occasionally. Sometimes I will see lines or marks that I have never seen before. When this happens I look at all the lines and see if the mark or line is a break off of a line.

For, instance some of my clients have a short, deep line coming off the Life Line, either just under, or just over the Head Line. This is still a part of the Head Line and I read this as someone who has trouble making up their minds, as they have the ability to receive ideas from very different parts of their brain. They will often start and stop projects, but will eventually find their way to what works for them. This can be someone who was not able to go into the career they wanted as life events blocked their plans.

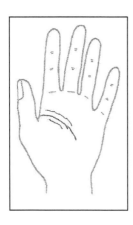

When there is a line above and below the Head Line, this is read as having dual thoughts and plans. For instance, this person could have gone to college with a plan in mind, dropped out and worked for a time, then gone back and changed their minds again. They could have dual majors. I read for one gentleman who has two master degrees in very different areas of studies and his main career wasn't in either of them. Then, when he was in his forties, he went back to school and focused on yet another degree and he now works in this field.

If there are more than two short Head Lines coming off the Life Line, and I have seen people with up to five, it is someone who truly is a jack of all trades and a master of none. I look at the other lines in the hand and if there are nice deep lines in a practical hand, I tell the client that it is OK to try many avenues of interest as they can succeed in all of them. If the hand has lighter lines, and a soft texture I tell them to make lists of what they hope to accomplish. This person will try one idea and stop, then pick up another idea or skill and drop that. They don't get much accomplished in the scheme of things.

This is not to say these people aren't talented people. Each of those lines can represent a talent or a natural ability. But, they won't get as much accomplished if they don't work on them one at a time.

Dots and Dashes

Dots on the palm are usually red or brown. If it is a dark mark from a pencil that went into the palm in grade school, it is not read. If it is a dark mark from a mole, it is not read, but this person should have their physician check out the mole.

A red dot is read by Oriental palmists as money coming into the person's life. If it is in the area above the Heart Line, or on the Mount of Venus, it is marrying money. Not to be read as marrying for money. If it is in other parts of the hand, it will be ideas and work that make the money.

Any line that crosses a line is called a dash and they are read as part of the line or Mount where they are situated. They are often good news. Think of them as messengers of good tidings. Under the Apollo finger it is good news around a creative project. Under the Jupiter it is good news regarding a business or job. Head Line, good ideas coming from your imagination, and connected with the Mercury Mount it means good news around a communication project.

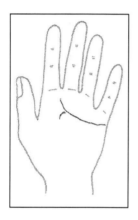

When there is a line that comes off the Heart Line, under the Mount of Jupiter, or between the Mount of Jupiter and the Mount of Saturn and it drops down towards the Head Line, it is someone who is fretting or brooding about something that has already happened, or is currently going on in their lives. This is a negative trend, and I tell people with this to whistle or sing when they brood about something they can't do anything about. It becomes a habit of self-pity, resulting in anger or depression and this is not good for you. Self-pity is a deadly emotion and, in my opinion, it leads to serious illness. When bad things happen to you; feeling sorry for yourself keeps the negative energy around you all the time. Handle the emotion and let it go. Don't try and figure out why something happened to you, you aren't going to know. Just build a bridge and get over it. Snap your fingers, whistle or sing when you begin to brood. Do this action every time and you will teach your brain to quit doing this.

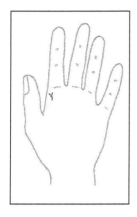

The pilots' line looks like a Y, and it is usually on the Mount of Jupiter. I read this literally as someone who can or will learn to fly planes or navigate ships. I also read this symbolically as someone who is presented with an opportunity that is good, but perhaps they think it is more than they can handle. They will not let their fears stop them from navigating themselves into a position of authority. When this is on the Mount of Luna they are navigating their ideas into a position where they can be used. When the pilot's line is situated in the second phalange of the thumb (the education area) this is someone who isn't going to let fear stop them from learning new skills. This can also be someone who is in school to learn to fly.

Stick Figures

I have seen this only rarely and the one client that comes to mind is a wonderful woman who has three children and five grandchildren. This year, on the Mount of Jupiter, I saw five small stick figures. This meant her five grandchildren were on her mind because of something exciting she was planning for them. In this case it was a gift she planning to give them. I didn't immediately think grandchildren when I saw them, but they looked like young beings, so I assumed that is what they meant and it was correct. Where ever the stick figure appears in the hand, it does relate to people in the person's life. If it is on the Mount of Venus they are holding their loved one in their heart, if on the Mount of Luna, they are dedicating some project or money to their loved one. I have only seen stick figures on the Mount of Jupiter, but I know they can be anywhere.

Angels

I have recently been seeing angels in the palms and this has meant that the person I am reading for has lost someone dear to them. The angel is not the person who has died; they have somehow called the angel to them to help them with their grief. I usually ask the person I am reading for if they have lost someone in their lives. I don't want to predict death, it wouldn't be good for me and my clients would hate it. If I am not sure where I am in time, I ask my client if this has already happened. That is not to say the angel couldn't be there as a different sort of protection, because it could. I have had some clients respond with, "Oh, that is my grandmother; I know she is a guardian angel now." I personally believe that angels are a different species from humans. I believe our deceased loved ones are always with us on some level, but they usually don't hang around to watch over us. They have busy lives on the other side.

Winged Beasts and Mythical Creatures

I also see mythical creatures, winged beasts, and dragons in the Mount of Luna. This has been happening in the past few years and it is someone who either writes fantasy, or plays a lot of computer games with fantasy creatures in them. I read for some pretty imaginative writers who are published in the fantasy genre and they create a world that shows up in their hands. I read for a lot of writers, and so far I haven't been able to see that clearly in the hands of those who write murder and mayhem stories. Thank goodness!

I have seen bombs going off and carnage in the palms of soldiers. I tell them they have to find a way to put those visions and feelings in storage. Your brain is like a computer and it is designed to process and store. We don't want to be processing bad things. It is possible to store the bad things and think about only good things.

Hard to Read Palms

If you come across palms that have lines running every which way and they just don't seem to be where they are supposed to be, begin by finding the major lines. Trace them in the hand and read them. Then look at the mounts, read them and then add in any lines that double and triple. Don't panic, some people have convoluted hands, but you can interpret any hand by learning the lines, the meanings and finding where they fit in the hand you are looking at. Just keep looking, following where a line begins and ends. Even in the most difficult hand, the fingers and mounts are where they should be and that should help you figure out the rest of the major lines. Whatever you say and do; DO NOT TELL THEM THAT YOU CAN'T READ FOR THEM. This sticks in their head forever. They remember this, and think they are negative people, or they are going to die soon. Don't do this to anyone.

When I read at busy shows I talk fast and I say a lot. One time I took a deep breath before starting reading for a lady. The following year she came back to me and told me she worried all year about what I didn't say because of that deep breath. I now explain that I am taking a breath because I need the breath.

CHAPTER 11

IN A NUTSHELL

You hold your life in the palms of your hands. You hold the secrets of your past, present and future in the palms of your hands. Your major lines are there to show how you think and the minor lines are there to tell you how you are living your life. Your future comes as a result of the decisions you are making now and have made in the past. If you don't like your present, change the way you think, make new decisions and your life changes. The future changes as well. Some parts of our lives are pre-destined, but for most of us our lives depend on our choices.

Louise Hay said, "I do not fix the problems in my life, I fix my life, and the problems fix themselves."

I have clients who explain why they are having an un-happy life. They tell me their childhood was awful. One of my favorite bumper stickers says, "It is never too late to have a happy childhood." Childhood is only eight-een years of our lives. Don't keep recreating your childhood. Go forward and make your future happy.

If you, as a palmist, or just someone reading the palms of your friends and family, can help someone see that they can make their life whatever they wish it to be; that is a remarkable thing and you have helped someone re-shape their destiny.

CHAPTER 12

YOUR RESPONSIBILITES
AS A PALM READER

You have responsibilities as a palm reader. I have already mentioned some of these responsibilities in the earlier chapters, but here are some more. Take your responsibilities as a palm reader, whether professional or amateur, seriously.

It is important to realize that you can be wrong. You can interpret the lines incorrectly, so learn all the ways to interpret them.

Respect the other person's right to disagree with you. You can tell them what their hand says, and they can tell you that you are wrong. Some clients love to do this. When someone does this to me, I tell them that this is what their palm says, and then I read the line again with an alternative meaning. Sometimes it is the way I have phrased my statements that make them think I am wrong. Show compassion to your clients and do not be judgmental. They are choosing to come to you because they want to hear what you have to say. Sometimes they are there just for fun and sometimes it is someone who really needs your help.

Be prepared to hear their stories and don't dismiss their problems, even if their problems seem like small problems to you.

Keep your sense of humor and, lastly, find your universal love energy and share this energy with your client.

Do not scare your client with your readings and don't project your life, or your hopes and dreams into your readings. For instance: I know a reader who is a single mother, and she predicts that her clients will be single mothers if their lines are at all similar to hers. This is wrong, both because it is steering the client, and because there really isn't a line that predicts single motherhood. The palm reader is projecting. Why would you want to steer a young woman in that direction? This is simply ego talking.

154

CHAPTER 13

QUESTIONS FROM CLIENTS

Will I have a happy life?

Happiness is really up to the individual. I read for people who have terrible things happen to them, and to their loved ones. Yet, they are still very happy people. I read for other people who seem to have had a life that is easier than most, and they are miserable. The path way to happiness is finding your inner passion in life and doing it. This inner passion doesn't have to come from your career; it can be from a hobby. Happiness is living your life with humor, dignity and honor. Happiness is caring enough about yourself to let only people who are kind and loving stay in your life. It is not what happens in your life that makes you happy or sad; it is how you choose to deal with what happens to you that makes your life happy or sad.

If you are unhappy because your mental health is poor, you can change this with medicine or therapy. Don't let yourself stay unhappy. Life is to be lived.

When am I going to die?

Contrary to most of the old books, the life line doesn't tell you how long you are going to live. I have had clients and members of my family die and it has never shown in the life line. In fact, it has never shown in the palm. I suspect the length of life is in the Rachettes, and I choose not to learn read this.

This is something that most of us are not supposed to know. If you are supposed to know, God will tell you. I don't choose to be the kind of reader who foretells death.

What happens when you die?

There are times during a reading when I can see a deceased relative or friend. There are always other people around them to help them make the transition between life and death. There are times when I see or hear that these people are other family members and I can describe them. There are times in a reading when I get messages from their loved one. There seems to be levels of life on the other side. There seems to be no time as we know it on the other side. The message I get again and again for my client is; they need to grieve and then get on with their lives. Their loved ones are busy and happy on the other side.

I don't purposely try to be a medium when I read palms. But there is an empathy that develops between me and the person I am reading for. I feel their pain and I desire to help them feel better. This triggers the mechanism within my brain that allows me to see and hear from the person they have lost.

What is my purpose?

I believe that most of our lives are free will and what happens to us comes from choices we have made, and are making. For instance, say you live one hundred years, and now you are dead and you are looking at a graph of your life. What a shock to find out that only five minutes of your life was fated and here you were spending all of your time on earth waiting for life to bring you your fate. You wasted all your other minutes waiting for life to happen to you. Maybe ten years were fated, maybe a month. You won't know until you are dead. You have to assume your entire life depends on the choices you make. When you take responsibility for your choices and for your life; you get sick of making choices that constantly cause you pain.

Yes, fated events can happen to us. Frequently, someone who has had an accident, or a death or some other traumatic event, will tell me that they don't know what they are supposed to learn from this. What is the lesson in this event? Quit trying to figure out why. Just go through the healing process and heal. When you are dead you can look at the graph of life and then you can say, "That is why that happened." But for now, just baby yourself and heal.

Do I have a soul mate? Is my current partner my soul mate?

If you have lived many lives you have many soul mates. Some are your friends, some are your family. Not all soul mates are on the same spiritual path as you are, and they wouldn't suit you in this life. When it is the right soul mate for you, the timing is right; meaning you are relatively close in age, and you both feel the connection. It is not the soul mate for you if it is someone who treats you badly. The timing is not right if the other person is married, or living with someone else. You may be deeply attracted to someone who isn't right for you, or who doesn't reciprocate your feelings. This isn't the soul mate you should be in love with. Don't get caught up in the "poor me, I am going to love them forever even if they dump all over me" mentality. Learn to let the people who treat you badly go, and move on. Find someone you can be happy with; someone who treats you well and loves you back.

When am I going to be happy?

This is like the question, "Am I going to have a happy life?" Happiness depends on you as well. No one can make you happy, but you. Nothing can make you happy. Millions of dollars can't. I read for some very wealthy people who are severely unhappy and some very poor people who radiate happiness. Marriage can't make you happy, and neither can children, or things that you buy. Happiness comes from finding hobbies and passions that make you so excited about your life that you can't wait to wake up each morning. Happiness comes from within.

If you can't find happiness because of mental illness, there are therapists and treatments available to you. Don't be afraid or ashamed to find what it takes to fix your life.

CHAPTER 14

HOW TO PICK A READER

Picking a reader is an instinctive process. Pick a reader who feels right to you. Don't go to one that feels wrong to you.

Years ago I went to a palm reader and she seemed very good. However, at the end of the reading she told me that a curse had been put on me, and that is why I was having troubles (I don't even remember what my troubles were). She needed to have money to take the curse off. The money wasn't for her, she assured me, it was for the Bible-some readers tell their clients the money is to be burned- the Lord needed the act of me giving her money to take the curse off. THIS IS A SCAM. WALK AWAY.

You should feel warmth and kindness from the person who is doing your reading.

When you go to a reader you have the right to expect that they will be honorable to you. Look at the signs the reader uses to advertise their profession. I was told to stay away from palmists who have a red or black hand on their sign. I also stay away from readers who are in private homes with neon signs out front, and ones who are in store fronts. If the reader is at a bookstore you are more likely to have a reader who is accountable, and most Renaissance Festivals are a good place to find readers as they have been juried in. Trust your intuition when you pick a reader.

If you go to a reader, and you don't feel comfortable after a few minutes, bring the reading to an end and walk away.

If you go to a reader and you have agreed on a set price and they want more money to add more to the reading; walk away. This is also a scam.

Lastly, be skeptical of anything the reader tells you until you recognize it as your truth.

CHAPTER 15

HOW DO I KNOW
IF I AM PSYCHIC?

Do you think about someone you haven't seen for a long time and you either run into them or they call you within a day or two?

Do you dream in color? Do you have dreams that come true? Do you wake up hearing someone talking to you as if they are reading from a book?

Have you ever had a feeling that you should not do something, or you should do something and when you didn't follow your intuition, you regretted it?

Do you have synchronicity? This can be fun as you always find a good parking spot. This is being in the right spot at the right time and people with a lot of synchronicity are often very lucky in games of chance.

Or you may have enough electrical energy that machines break when you are using them. You go through cell phones and even laptop computers at an alarming rate. Sometimes these people can't wear a watch as they always stop.

This is all part of psychic energy.

We all have some psychic ability. Most people just never acknowledge it. They prefer to say that they are a good judge of people, or they have hunches. Well, the ability to read people accurately is using psychic intuition and so is following your hunches. There are many ways people 'just know things'. An older lady I know always knew when company was coming and even who was coming. She would see a crow in the yard, or she dropped a fork and it was turned towards the door.

Each sign had a meaning to her; these were her vehicles or her methods of 'divination'.

Divination is the art that seeks to foresee or foretell future events by the interpretation or insight, into a question or situation by way of a standardized process.

Thus, the interpretations of the meanings of the lines of the hand become a standardized process. You tap into your own intuition, or psychic energy, which taps into the energy of the person you are reading, and this is how you get an intuitive palm reading. This works for any other type of reading as well.

Psychic energy waves obey the laws of physics just like radio waves, light waves or sound waves. They come from a different end of the spectrum. We can't hear sound or see light beyond a certain range, but various types of instruments and machines can pick up that energy from a long distance. They can also transmit it. Radios, cell phones and television do it all the time. Right now psychic energy can't be measured, although, people are trying to.

I have met a lot of wonderful people in the last forty years. I have met and talked with hundreds of psychics, and I notice they often seem scattered or burned out. Their personal lives are a mess, and while they help others, they can't always help themselves. I realized that their own intuition was doing them a disservice. They were using their psychic ability to help everyone else and they were absorbing or taking on everyone's problems. I decided that I didn't want to be like that. This doesn't mean my life is without problems, because you can't live a life without challenges. But I believe we can be psychic and happy. When my life goes mad, I stop and fix it. I can still read for other people, I am able to turn my psychic energy on or tone it down when necessary.

The following chapters are my journey into the psychic world and the exercises I use to keep centered and grounded.

CHAPTER 16

JOURNEY INTO THE CENTER
OF BEING PSYCHIC

My Psychic Journey

I had a psychic experience that forever changed my life. I was newly single and I 'saw' a man climbing into the hall window of my house. I told my friends and my counselor and they all agreed it was just fear as I wasn't used to living alone. This occurred for three nights and the fourth night a man did climb through a window in my home. It was a different window and he was dressed differently than in my vision. I thought at first that I made this happen. By seeing this I believed I had brought this to me. I believed by seeing it, I had created it.

Fortunately, this man was caught and went to jail. The event, while traumatic, could have been worse. But believe me, if I ever have a vision like this again, I would lock my windows and get a security alarm.

I discussed this vision with many people and finally someone said, "You have ESP! You were having a psychic experience."

This began my psychic journey. I began reading everything I could on psychic phenomenon. I met a young Indian woman who had learned to read palms from her grandmother and she shared with me what she knew. I took classes, and studied with an American Indian Shaman as well as many other people.

I had no intentions of reading palms for anyone else but my friends and family, but fate had other plans for me. I went to a company Christmas party with a friend, who is now my husband of thirty seven years, and he told everyone there that I read palms. I said, "No, I don't." But, I read for everyone there and this began my career as a palm reader. By necessity, I learned to control my psychic ability.

As I said in an earlier chapter, I would end my palm reading with a hand clasp that connected the web between my thumb and forefinger with the web between their thumb and forefinger. I closed my eyes and did a sort of stream of consciousness reading. I saw pictures of what the person was doing just before they came to me. That was interesting, even exciting.

I then decided I would visualize a light gray cloud above the head of the person I was reading. I would throw my mind ahead of that cloud to see if I could see the future, focusing on whatever my client was asking questions about. I did get visual impressions and I saw coming events this way. At times I would get dates and times.

This was exciting. People would come back in a few days and tell me that I was correct, that what I had predicted had occurred.

After a few days of doing this, I noticed that I was hearing a buzzing in the corner of the room, near the ceiling. At first it sounded like a mosquito and later in the day it sounded like a wasp. The next day the buzz began to sound like a record at high speed, and the following day it sounded like a record at slow speed. Fortunately the show ended, and I decided to do some research to see what this noise could be.

What I found gave me goose bumps. When an entity tries to speak to you, this is what it will sound like in the beginning. Your brain is trying to tune in the entities voice; at first you hear it at too fast a speed and then later too slow. The next step would be to actually hear the voice. This voice was outside my head. I think all of us have a voice that speaks to us inside our head. The inner voice may be our subconscious or our higher conscious or our spirit guide, but it is not a discarnate (doesn't come from a physical body) voice. The voice in the corner of the room was a discarnate voice, and maybe it could also be a voice from a spirit guide, but I really didn't want that. I felt, and still feel, that this would be too much for me to handle.

Because of this, I studied ways to open and shut my psychic doors and ways to control how open I allow myself to be. I don't want to hear voices outside of my head. I work very hard to stay centered, grounded and in control at all times.

I also noticed that I was picking up other people's energy, and I was feeling burned out, agitated or drained by the end of the day. I worked as a waitress in a bar serving lunches and I began to feel ill by the end of my shift. I couldn't figure out what was going on until my usual bartender was out sick for a week. I felt good for that week. I was feeling my usual high energy. When the bartender came back to work I felt ill again. Finally, I realized that I was picking up his illness.

One day, at a fair an American Indian man came to me and told me he was guided to give me some pointers on how to center and ground my psychic energy so that I wouldn't burn out. He told me I had a talent that needed to be used for many years. I listened to what he said, and immediately incorporated these exercises into my daily routine. After a few weeks I didn't pick up my bartenders illness anymore. I later found out he was an alcoholic and the days I felt so bad, he had been coming off a binge.

I don't want to become scattered and burned out. I don't want to pick up negative energy from people around me. I have learned to keep other people's energy at enough of a distance from me that I keep myself clear. Joseph Campbell wrote, "The psychic swims in the waters the psychotic drowns in." We all want to swim and not drown in this energy.

Exercises in Centering and Grounding

These are the exercises that were given to me by an American Indian Shaman. He came out of a crowd of people at the Minnesota Renaissance Festival and told me to do this visualization several times a day so I would not burn out when using my psychic gifts to help my clients.

Imagine yourself in a golden magic ball. It is a bubble. It surrounds you. It is clear, you can breathe through it and you can see through it. Mine is an amber color, but it must be a shade of yellow. If you can't visualize a ball, spread your arms out and draw the bubble around you. Inside the ball the air smells wonderful, fresh, like an elixir. The air smells of your favorite fragrance. Mine is fresh pine. Your bubble is magic. You are safe and protected in the ball. It is yours.

Imagine a golden magic cord draped loosely around your shoulders. It is connecting you to God. This brings your shoulders up, you feel positive and surrounded by love.

Imagine a golden magic cord loosely draped around your ankles. This cord is connecting you to the earth. This is a grounding cord and it is vital. You are now centered between heaven and earth and you feel perfect in your bubble.

Do this visualization every day, many times a day. It took me about five months to realize the full benefit of this exercise. You aren't shutting yourself off psychically or emotionally from the people you love. You are telling your higher conscious mind that you have boundaries, and to put those boundaries in place. I find that I feel quieter in my thoughts and more settled in my solar plexus when I have my boundaries in place.

Opening and Closing the Psychic Centers

No one really knows exactly where the psychic center is in the body. Some feel it is the crown chakra, the seventh chakra, which is at the top of the head. Others feel

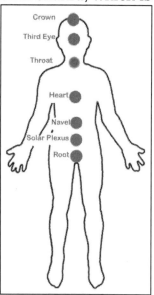

it is in the forehead, the sixth chakra, which is also called the third eye. Others feel it is the throat chakra, which is the fifth chakra, or the heart chakra, which is the fourth chakra, or the solar plexus which is the third chakra. I feel that each of the chakras, including the second and first are psychic receptors; depending on the type of psychic energy you are using. I know when I have done a lot of readings I feel a pull at the third eye. I also know that I pull in energy through my crown chakra and send it out through my heart chakra. When I have been doing too many readings I feel it in my throat chakra and I feel it in the solar plexus. I do exercises to open these chakras and I do exercise to close them at the end of my day.

I used to imagine huge metal furnace doors over each of my chakras at the end of a day and at the beginning of the day I would imagine them open.

To make an impact on my mind, I would use my hands to draw open the furnace doors. I would close them the same way. You will automatically open your psychic doors, and automatically close them eventually. You will feel when this is happening. At that time you would not need to do this exercise. But until then, practice opening your chakra manually by either visualizing them open or drawing them open with your hands. At the end of your sessions, manually close them. Make a production of drawing them open at the beginning of your day and closing them at the end of the day. This makes an impact on your subconscious mind. You are patterning your brain just as you pattern muscles and this is called muscle memory, which is an athlete's term. After all, your brain is just a muscle.

Most of the psychic energy that I use comes through my third eye. The third eye is constructed much the same way our other eyes are. You can't see the third eye, but imagine it has a pupil, or some type of sensing ability that dilates when it senses light. When the third eye is too open, it is much like when you go to an eye doctor and he puts drops in your eyes. Your pupils get enlarged and there is too much light. You need very dark sun glasses to see anything. When the pupil of the third eye is too open you have no psychic vision either. You are taking in too much light. It is as if you are a radio that is turned on, and not tuned in.

I was given this exercise in a meditation. Every day I say, "I am closed psychically, unless I can save someone's life." I urge you to do this too, as part of your routine. Open your chakras and then say this aloud. People don't want to do this as they feel they will shut off their intuition. This exercise is like putting on sun glasses in a bright light. Your psychic vision actually becomes clearer. Your pupil is narrowing, and you won't pick up randomly from everyone you come in contact with. I don't believe in wasting the psychic energy. I read for people who have lists of all the natural disasters they are picking up, or other terrible world events. This does no one any good. You can't change these events by knowing them in advance, so what is the point? Each one of us has the power to change a small portion of our lives. Narrow your psychic vision and change what you can change. Let God take care of what you can't change.

Breathing Exercises

Breathing is important to bring oxygen to your cells. Needless to say, smoking isn't something anyone should do, but it is vital for a psychic not to smoke. It is also important to be sober when you are practicing your psychic ability. In the sixties and seventies, I knew people who used various types of drugs to enhance their psychic energy. It didn't work. What they picked up was garbled, weird and made no sense to themselves or the people they were reading for. As a side note: the people I know who used a lot of drugs, even marijuana, lost their dreams along the way. Some of them can go to the same movie again and again and it is fresh each time, as their memories aren't that good. Don't do this to yourself.

These are the breathing exercises I do each day.

During the breathing exercises I take the time to count my blessings, and give thanks for them.

Every morning when you wake up, take a few minutes to stand with your head raised and your shoulders back. Bring your arms out in front of you and take a deep breath. Then swing your arms out and around to your back while exhaling. Begin by doing these four or five times each morning, going up to ten breaths after a few days. You can do this at night as well.

Next, find a spot in your home where you can sit quietly. Close your eyes and take a few deep calming breaths. Inhale slowly; hold for a few seconds and exhale slowly. While doing this, visualize your life. Look at your blessings, mentally list them and give thanks for them. At night when you do this, look at one of your problems and visualize it solved. Do each problem individually, focusing on it and then visualize it solved.

For the next exercise stand upright again. Make sure your shoulders are back and your spine is straight. Hold the right nostril closed with your right hand and breathe in slowly to the count of ten. Hold your breath to the count of ten while visualizing the oxygen coming into your lungs and then moving into your spine adding rich oxygen to your spinal fluid. Visualize the air moving down your spine and going around your tail bone. As the air reaches your tail bone and begins its journey up the spine and into the lungs, hold the left nostril closed with your left hand and breathe out to the count of ten. Do this again holding the left nostril closed with your left hand and breathing out holding your right nostril closed with your right hand. Do this three times and work up to eight to ten times a day. If this makes you dizzy, lower your count to five.

Now take a deep breath through your nose. Make sure this deep breath goes into your stomach. Bring it to the depth of your stomach until your stomach is extended. Hold for the count of four and then let the breath out through your mouth. Do this at least five times.

Remember, breathe blessings in in the morning and exhale problems out in the evenings.

CHAPTER 17

THE FIRST FIVE SENSES

We all are aware of our five senses, which are the senses of sight, smell, hearing, touch and taste. We use all of them in different combinations to experience our life and to make decisions every day without any thought. If one is suddenly taken away it takes a long time to learn to compensate for the loss. You wouldn't think that you would use your sense of sight to taste but when you watch people doing taste tests when blindfolded it is amazing that they often fail to identify common foods.

To become more aware of our sixth sense, it is important to exercise our other five senses as well. The following exercises help you to tune in to your senses, thus strengthening the sixth sense.

Strengthening the First Five

The Sense of Sight

When you are out and about during the day, whether at work or just playing, take a few seconds to really see what is around you. If you are outdoors, look at the colors in the vegetation; really examine the textures on the buildings you are looking at. Look at the shading where the sun hits the buildings. When I am in painting classes my instructor tells me to cross my eyes to see the negative space, the space around objects. Do this when you are doing your sight exercises.

I have friends who are able to see something and draw it. I always thought perhaps their vision was different from mine, that they had a different perspective than I had. I bought some of the gold sunglasses that are advertised on television and when I wear them I do see differently. If I look at a large grove of trees on the side of the road with my regular glasses I see a lot of green in various heights and shapes. When I use the sunglasses, each tree is clearly defined and the different shades of green stand out from each other. I believe that is how natural artists see. We are trying to define our world more clearly with the sight exercises.

While you are doing your observing exercises, try and separate the things you are looking at; carefully observe the shapes and the colors. Say out loud, "I am training my mind to see clearly with my physical eyes and my psychic eyes."

At night, turn off the lights and look around you. At first you will only see blobs in the darkness. As your eyes adjust to less light, you see shapes and forms. Again, say out loud, "I am learning to see clearly with my physical eyes and my psychic eye."

Have someone make a tray with ten objects on it. Have them cover it and then you take the cover off, look at it for two minutes. Cover the tray and list what was on the tray. When you are able to recall each item, add more items. This is done at showers today, but it is an excellent exercise to sharpen your observation skills. It also helps with visualization. If you visualize what is on the tray you can more easily remember each item.

There are two kinds of psychic sight. One is seeing people or events in the mind and the other is seeing visions outside the mind in the real world. These often appear as hologram like images.

I am able to see in both ways. When I read palms I see images in the palms. Sometimes the lines form the images and sometimes they just form on their own.

I have occasionally seen ghosts and other entities, but I don't seek this out. When this happens I say out loud, "What are you doing here and what do you need me to do?" Do I get answers? Sometimes. But this is for another book.

A little aside about discarnate energy, which includes ghosts and other energies: You, as a human being in a material body, control this space. The other energies don't. You can tell them to go away in a commanding voice and they must listen. The fear you often feel when in the presence of this type of energy makes the hair on your arms stand up and you feel a cold chill that runs up your spine. You are not necessarily really afraid; it is that this type of energy vibrates at a frequency that triggers the fear response in your body. But enough of this, I will do another book about how to see and hear from the other side at another time.

The Sense of Smell

You wouldn't think that the sense of smell has any value in the psychic world, but it does. Some psychics swear that they smell a veritable potpourri of scents around people, and that is how they do their readings. They may use a different vehicle, such as palms or cards, but they smell their readings. This is not something I do, but occasionally I will smell a certain fragrance when I see ghost energy. Usually they smell something like fresh baked cookies.

To strengthen the sense of smell is important, as it is an important part of our senses. To do this, open a container of spice in your kitchen and take a light whiff. See if you can identify it. Close your eyes and have a friend hold different spices to your nose and see if you can identify them. Then, when you are eating at someone's home, or in a restaurant, try and guess what spices are in the food you are eating. Wine connoisseurs are always conscious of the smells in the wine they are drinking. They say it enhances the taste of the wines and thus enhances their enjoyment of the drink.

Being more cognizant of the smells in the foods you eat may enhance your enjoyment of food.

Be aware of the scents on the air when you are outside.

I know massage therapists who smell a distinct smell when their clients are not healthy. It gets sharper when they have their hands on the area of the body that is unhealthy.

One of my teachers told me that she could smell death on someone who was going to die.

Sometimes you will smell a scent that indicates a paranormal event is taking place before you would feel their presence.

So each day, be aware of the smells around you. Sniff the air and identify them. Tell yourself out loud that you sensitizing your sense of smell so that your psychic sense will get stronger.

The Sense of Taste

When you are eating, take the time to chew your food. Don't drink while you have food in your mouth. Savor the flavors of each bite you take. Different parts of the tongue have sensors that taste different flavors. Take a moment to feel the texture of what you are eating.

Some people will have their mouth flood with a sweet taste when they encounter entities, others will have a bitter taste. Tell yourself that you are working on becoming more in tune with your sense of taste to help you become more psychic.

The Sense of Hearing

When you go to bed, lie quietly. Concentrate on all the sounds you hear and identify them. Perhaps you hear your refrigerator motor. Or rain on your roof.

Then expand on this, listen to your breathing, see if you can hear your heartbeat.

During the day, pay attention to all the sounds you hear for twenty minutes and identify them. Make it a habit to just sit in each room in your house and just listen.

As a psychic you may be auditory. Learning to listen can tune in your own psychic voice. The psychic voice is soft, but if you listen carefully and are aware of the ambient sounds, you may it. When you are in tune with your sense of hearing you will recognize when there is a sound that is unusual.

The Sense of Touch

The sense of touch is something you are very likely to encounter as a psychic.

If you decide to go into energy work such as healing by touch, or massage, you will need to have a very sensitive sense of touch. If you investigate the paranormal you usually sense entities by temperature changes before you would see or hear them. I touch the hands of the person I am reading, so touch is important in my work.

One way to sensitive your sense of touch is to have a cold object in one hand, and a hot or warm object in the other. Close your eyes and feel the difference in each object.

Put items of different textures in each hand. You can work with a friend and blindfold yourself or close your eyes, and see if you can identify what they put in your hands.

Keep your mind focused when you are doing each of the exercises to expand your senses.

Don't forget to give yourself the suggestion that you are working to sensitive your five senses to become more aware of your sixth sense.

CHAPTER 18
THE SIXTH SENSE

Our sixth sense is a natural part of all of us, yet we don't recognize it, and rarely use it when making important decisions in our lives.

It is often used in retrospect. Haven't you said, "I knew I shouldn't have done that?" Or "I knew I should have done that."

But how does it work?

Scientists are learning more and more about how our brain works. It is well known that the brain is an electrochemical organ; researchers have speculated that a fully functional brain can generate as much as ten watts of electrical power. The brain electricity can be measured by sensors placed on the scalp and they are displayed as brain waves. They vary in amplitude (height) and frequency. The number of waves per second is referred to as hertz or Hz.

There are four categories of brain wave patterns.

Beta (14-30 Hz although some charts say 15 to 40 Hz)

This is cognitive thought. These are the dominant brain frequencies when our eyes are open, when we are thinking and making decisions. This is a strongly engaged mind.

Higher levels are associated with anxiety, disease or the flight or fight response that we mammals have when threatened.

Alpha (8-13.9 some charts say 9-14 Hz)

This is relaxed thought, a light trance-the beginning of access to the sub-conscious mind. This is a walk in a garden, reading light fiction, painting a picture. This is the bridge between the conscious and the subconscious mind.

Theta (4-7.9 Hz some charts say 5-8 HZ)

This can also be achieved with deep relaxation techniques and hypnosis. These brain wave patterns are connected with creativity, intuition and daydreaming. This is also what happens when you are driving on the freeway and you can't recall the past thirty minutes. This is also a state of mind you can achieve with prayer and meditation.

Delta (.1-3.9 also 1.5 to 4 Hz)

The higher numbers are dreaming sleep and the lowest numbers are dreamless sleep.

It is a loss of physical awareness. Dreaming sleep numbers can be induced with deep trance mediation. This is the place where we can experience the collective consciousness of the universe.

The deeper sleep is only achieved during dreamless sleep.

There are other brain frequencies that occur above 30Hz but I will not refer to them except to comment that perhaps this is the person whose mind spins or shows a lot of anxiety. They think too much. These numbers may be a person who can't relax their mind enough to sleep. This may also be what kids and adults show with attention deficit disorder. But these numbers don't apply to what I am trying to show you.

I believe that I achieve the alpha state of mind when I am reading palms. I also believe that I occasionally hit the theta state and even the light delta state when I am reading for long periods of time. I know that when I am reading I don't feel my body. I also achieve the alpha state of mind when I am sculpting and painting. This is the state of mind that runners and swimmers call the 'high' they achieve when they are in the 'zone' with their sport.

The exercises we are doing are going to help you find and achieve that state of mind. It is the place where you can work on your problems and achieve success.

In order to access the intuitive or psychic part of the brain we need to achieve at least the alpha state, and later the theta state, and remain there without going to sleep.

I have never worked with a biofeedback machine. I don't know how to tell if the ones being sold are real or a scam so I stay away from them. I think if you could see your mind going into an alpha, or a theta state it would be easier to achieve. I learned to reach my alpha and theta states of mind on trust. Trust that if I practiced my relaxation techniques and my visualization techniques, I would strengthen my psychic ability. It worked for me; it can work for you too.

The following are exercises that I use. All you need to do to begin is to close your eyes and then practice. Practice is the key.

Relaxation Exercises

You may find that your best time to meditate is early in the morning. Or it may be at your lunch hour or in the evening. It doesn't matter, you have a unique energy system and you will find the time that works best for you. I prefer the evening for my meditation.

There are a multitude of books and tapes on meditating. Take a look at some of these. The following are exercises that I do.

Usually this exercise is done lying down, but if you are more comfortable sitting in a recliner, this will work too. Wear comfortable clothes and close your eyes. Tighten your right foot. Hold it tight for a few seconds and then relax it. Go to your left foot, tighten, hold and relax. Then tighten your calf muscles, hold and relax. Tighten your thigh muscles, hold and relax. Tighten your stomach and buttocks, hold and relax. Tighten your chest and back muscles, hold and relax. Tighten your arms, hold and relax. Tighten your neck, hold and relax. Tighten your head, hold and relax. Breathe deeply and slowly during the entire process of tightening the different zones of your body and relaxing them.

When I began using this exercise I did it with friends. They would talk me through the different exercises, and as I progressed and started to see things at the different levels, they would take notes. The first times you do this don't try and see anything. You are working to deepen your consciousness; you are going to a deeper level of your mind. You can do this with someone, a psychic buddy, although doing it alone works just as well.

If visualizing is difficult for you, cut something out of a magazine. It can be anything that catches your eye. Look at it for several minutes and then close your eyes and reconstruct it from your memory. Do this with different pictures before you do the exercises below. Remember, if you can see it, you can believe it and you can achieve it.

While you are relaxed, visualize yourself at the top of a cliff with stairs going down. You are outdoors and it is evening. The weather is lovely and there is a slight breeze. The stars are out and the moon is full enough to see clearly. There is no fear in this place. Tell yourself that you are going to walk down the stairs and that with each step you will become more and more relaxed. (If you need a railing on the stairs to be comfortable, visualize the railing.) Each step you take brings you to a different level of consciousness. Start at the number ten and slowly count down to one. Take a deep breath as you say each number in your count down. When you hit one, you are on a platform and this platform is a resting place. Later, when you are confident with this relaxation exercise, you can explore what is on the platforms. You can tell yourself that you will find the answers to whatever questions you need answered while you are on the platforms.

But for now, just continue working your way down the cliff. Each ten steps is another platform and each step takes you deeper and deeper into your subconscious mind.

If you fall asleep doing this exercise, don't be upset. Even in sleep you are learning to access your subconscious mind at will.

I have also done the same exercise with the visualization that I was in an elevator going down and a different one in an elevator going up. Watch the elevator monitor. Each floor that you go down is taking you down to a deeper level of relaxation. If you use the elevator going up, then each floor still takes you into a deeper layer of meditation.

Pick the visualization that you are comfortable with and do this every day. But do go at least one hundred steps or floors.

When this is easy to do, pose a question you want answered or ask for a healing at each level. Explore each platform or floor on the way down or on the way up. Really take the time to look around at each level. Note the colors you see. Note how you feel.

When I am in the alpha state I feel light hearted and euphoric. I don't feel my body, yet my brain feels hyper-alert. I don't mean nervous when I say hyper-alert either. I mean that I am aware of all the vibrations and colors that are around me. I am in tune with the universe.

After doing this exercise often enough that it is fairly easy to do, tell yourself you can achieve this same level of relaxation by closing your eyes, taking four deep breaths and counting to four.

If you feel you are hitting negative thoughts or vibrations on any of the platforms or floors, build a wall around that floor and then discard it. Stop on a different set of numbers. For instance, if the negative vibrations hit you at the eighth floor or platform; wall it off and stop at eight and a half. This is your visualization. You own it and you are always in control.

Each time you do this you are opening up to a greater awareness of you. You are working to open your mind to enlightenment, fulfillment, self-knowledge and self-realization. It takes time and patience to really achieve an alpha state or a theta state, but you can do it.

Visualization

First do the technique of tightening and relaxing your body. Then do four deep slow breaths. Inhaling slowly to the count of six and exhaling to the count of six.

Now close your eyes and visualize yourself as you are. Construct your body from the crown of your head to the soles of your feet. See yourself as clearly as you can. Hold that image, and then imagine your neck elongating. Your neck is strong enough to hold your head no matter what, but it can stretch like Rubber Man in the comics. You are stretching your head above the ceiling in your room; imagine going through the ceiling as if the ceiling is mist. Imagine yourself going through the roof as if it, too, is mist. If this is hard to do, imagine yourself out of doors. Soon your head is above the clouds and you are streaking towards the moon. Let yourself feel the freedom. You are comfortable; you are in tune with all things. Visualize what the clouds feel like on your skin. Really look at them. Make a note of how far down it is to your toes and then slowly shrink your neck back to where it belongs.

When I began trying to see the future for my clients I would have them ask a question and I would visualize raising my head above my body and then throwing it into the question and the future. This worked; it did give me a headache at first, even though I didn't really throw my physical head anywhere.

You should do this exercise a few times each week. You can stretch any part of your body. Visualize stretching your arms out as far as you can visualize them. Then stretch your body from the waist up, then your body from your feet up.

Now shrink yourself down to the size of an ant. You are tiny. See everything as larger than you are. Look to see if you can identify anything when you are that small. Really get into this exercise. Visualize everything in the room you are in. Now make yourself bigger, the size of a mouse. Visualize everything in the room the size it would be if you were a mouse.

Changing the way you perceive your body in the universe helps open your consciousness to other realms of perception. It makes your mind more flexible.

Now bring yourself back into a relaxed state of being. Lie quietly and see yourself as a light. Project this light from the inner core of your being out into your aura. The energy field called your aura stretches out as far as your arms can stretch. Now visualize a dial sitting near your forehead that has numbers on it that run from one to ten. The number one is the lowest number and ten is the highest. You are on one and each day turn the number up one notch on the dial. Spend some time visualizing your light brighter, then turn the dial to back down to one. This is like turning the lights off in the room and it brings this visualization session to a close.

When you are in a relaxed state of mind you can visualize what you want to have happen in your life. You can use this to create a new life for yourself. You can program yourself in the alpha state to be more confident, to be thinner, to be more outgoing, or to quit smoking.

To really activate the program to make changes in your life you must really feel the need to change. You must have a great desire to make this happen. Your emotions need to be involved and then you do the visualization to make it happen.

CHAPTER 19

TRY A LITTLE CRYSTAL BALL MEDITATION

I do read the crystal ball for clients. It can also be used for a meditation exercise. You can use either a glass crystal ball or a natural quartz crystal ball for this exercise. You can also use a white bowl with clear water in it.

Sit in a comfortable position and have the crystal ball in front of you in such a way that it is relaxing to look at.

Sit and stare into the crystal ball, and try to blank out your thoughts. It is difficult to blank out our thoughts as they are constantly running around in our head. You can say a two syllable word over and over again to help you stop your thoughts and still your mind. The word ma-gic will work and so will fo-cus or ker-plunk. Find a two syllable sound that you like and keep saying it while you are staring into the crystal ball. Don't force your thoughts out of your mind, just take a deep breath and keep clearing out your thoughts and concentrate on the crystal.

You will start to see the ball getting darker and then lighter. Clouds will form, and then will move in and out of your crystal ball. Later, faces will form and they will seem to swim in and out of the crystal ball.

You are getting into the alpha state when the faces appear. I have taught crystal ball reading and the faces differ with each person. I see faces that seem to be Arabic; dark men and veiled women, or American Indian men and women. Some of my students reported seeing faces that were dressed in pirate clothing, others Colonial America. Everyone has different experiences.

When the faces clear out, the ball will go dark for a time and then the ball lights up and you will see visions. At this juncture, my crystal ball has a small section that lights up, not the entire ball, and I see moving pictures. Have a tape recorder handy to document what you see.

This takes a long time to master, so be patient; but while you are mastering it, you are teaching yourself to go into the alpha state and then the theta state. You have to be in the theta state to see visions in the crystal ball.

CHAPTER 20

PUTTING THE PALM AND THE PSYCHIC TOGETHER

Psychic thought has a different feel than my other thoughts. I describe my psychic thought as thicker or denser than my other thoughts. My psychic thoughts have a weight to them.

When I taught psychic development I would tell my students to write down their intuitive or psychic thoughts and then be cognizant of how that thought felt. To describe how their psychic thought felt. Some described their psychic thought as a light, airy feel and some heard a tinkling of a bell. Everyone has a different way to describe the way psychic thought feels.

Become aware of your psychic thoughts, jot them in a notebook with the date, time and what you felt when you were thinking the thoughts. Go over your notebook frequently and check out your psychic thoughts. When you were right, remember how it felt to think that thought.

Once you have identified how your psychic thought comes through to you, you are closer to trusting and believing in your own abilities.

When I am reading palms I cross my eyes and squint into the palm. I do this when I am trying to project into the future for a prediction. For instance, if I do this when looking at the juncture of the Head Line and the Life Line, I can tell if someone will get a new job, a raise or a promotion. There will be a short feathery line that pops up. The closer it is to the Mount of Jupiter the closer the job opportunity is.

I do this when someone asks me a specific question. If it is about a new home, the area I look at is at the base of the wrist and the beginning of the Life Line. A small box appears, and when the box is open, it indicates a move. You may find that you see different symbols and they may be in a different place in the hand. It takes practice to interpret what you see and it also takes practice to see anything at all.

I also cross my eyes and look just above the person's head. This is where the aura is most easily seen. The aura is seen as bands of colors and it vibrates. I don't see the entire aura during a reading. I do see the vibrations of the aura and I see the first band as light or dark, clear or cloudy. If it is dark and cloudy it is usually a person who is using drugs, drinking too much, or is a heavy smoker. This is not a healthy person. It is occasionally someone who is very depressed. I do talk about this in a reading. I ask them if they use drugs, or of they smoke or drink. I ask them if they are depressed. I tell them it is time to quit their addictions. If they are depressed, I also tell them that they don't have to feel this way. They can fix this. I always say to myself, "Unless I can change something negative coming, I will not see it." So if I notice the aura or the vibrations as a dark energy, I know it is changeable and I tell my client that.

I have had clients who I have told to quit whatever they are doing that creates their dark aura, and they seem to listen. When I read for them some years later and the darkness is gone, I know either they have quit, or it is too late. I always feel very sad when I hear that a client has died of lung cancer or they are in chemo and radiation, when I know, had they listened to me years ago, this could have been avoided. Remember, I try and always see positive things, but if I see something negative, it is changeable.

When I read for couples I look over both of their heads. If they are vibrating in sync with each other it means they are on the same page in their spiritual growth. Usually this means they are a couple who will still be together in fifty or more years. If they are vibrating at different rates, I tell them that they need to keep finding things in common so they do stay on the same page throughout their lives. When I say, 'stay on the same page', I mean that in the book of our life, when we are on the same page with the person we love, there is a feeling of connecting that is deep and powerful. If you go on a different page you lose that connection and this leads to divorce. We all grow emotionally and spiritually throughout our lives, the trick with marriage is to grow together and not separately.

I also see a web over each person. It is gossamer and much like a spider web. This is the way our lives map out. It is made up of our decisions and as we do something new or make a new choice, an additional branch is spun out. This keeps branching out into infinity. I believe the web shows our probable future. If we do this, that will happen and if we do something else it leads to another branch, which opens up other probable futures. This goes on and on and on. When I am asked a question, after the initial palm reading, I look at the web until I can see the shiniest strand, and then I mentally pull on it. This is the most positive, probable outcome to their question and I will either see the answer or feel the answer.

We all have many strands of the web over our heads. But, I remember one time I read for a woman who was obviously very ill. I was having a hard time seeing a future for her in the hand. It looked like her life was just about over. I looked at the web above her head and most of the strands were shriveled up and dead looking. But there was one that looked shiny, so I pulled on it and saw that she would be getting well, and doing motivational speaking to other people who were coping with cancers like hers. This did come true and she told me years later that she kept focusing on what I had said when she felt like giving up. She felt that what I said had helped her get well. It may well be, but I believe she would have gotten well anyway because she had that one viable strand left.

On a few occasions I have seen a spinning metallic disk shape over my client's head. It looked like the disks you see on paintings of the saints and the holy family. This tells me that artists have also seen this disk in order for them to paint it. If you see a disk around someone this indicates a more evolved person. Evolved people can have problems too; they come to readers to get answers just like anyone else.

There are many mysterious and magical things that happen when you are studying and working with psychic energy. I find it exhilarating and comforting to know that there is much more to life than what we can see, taste, smell, feel or hear.

I am hoping that this book will lead you to find the magic and mystery in your life.

Psychic energy is used in healing of all types. It can be used in any type of work where you feed data into your brain and come to conclusions. Whatever and wherever you are in your life, your life will be enhanced by being in tune with and using your psychic ability.

6708937R00126

Made in the USA
San Bernardino, CA
13 December 2013